START & RUN A CREATIVE SERVICES BUSINESS

START & RUN A CREATIVE SERVICES BUSINESS

Susan Kirkland

Self-Counsel Press
(a division of)
International Self-Counsel Press Ltd.
USA   Canada

Self-Counsel Press acknowledges the financial support of the Government of Canada through the Book Publishing Industry Development Program (BPIDP) for our publishing activities.

Printed in Canada.

First edition: 2005

Second editon: 2009

Library and Archives Canada Cataloguing in Publication

Kirkland, Susan

    Start & run a creative services business / Susan Kirkland. — 2nd ed.

    ISBN 978-1-55180-864-2

    1. Home-based businesses. 2. New business enterprises.

    I. Title. II. Title: Start and run a creative services business.

    HD2333.K57 2008   658.1'141   C2008-906680-4

Acknowledgments

The lyrics from Bob Dylan's "She Belongs to Me" are Copyright© 1965 by Warner Bros. Inc. Copyright renewed 1993 by Special Rider Music. All rights reserved. International copyright secured. Reprinted by permission.

This book is printed in Canada on 100% post consumer waste Forest Stewardship Certified recycled paper, using plant-based inks. The paper is processed chlorine free and manufactured using biogas energy.

Recycled
Supporting responsible use of forest resources
www.fsc.org Cert no. SGS-COC-003153
© 1996 Forest Stewardship Council

Self-Counsel Press
(a division of)
International Self-Counsel Press Ltd.

1704 North State Street	1481 Charlotte Road
Bellingham, WA 98225	North Vancouver, BC V7J 1H1
USA	Canada

To Burris,
who taught me to see;

Trenney and McTish,
who shaped my voice;

Drummond and Link,
who taught me to think;

Myers,
who taught me good taste;

Blankenship,
for his generosity of spirit;

German,
for his tolerance;

W.A. Thomas,
my greatest friend, who never lost faith;

McCoy,
for his culpable sycophancy;

and Rosemary Chandler,
for her kindness.

She's got everything she needs,
She's an artist, she don't look back.
She can take the dark out of the nighttime
and paint the daytime black.
You will start out standing
Proud to steal her anything she sees.
But you will wind up peeking through her keyhole
Down upon your knees.
She never stumbles,
She's got no place to fall.
She's nobody's child,
The Law can't touch her at all.

—Bob Dylan, "She Belongs to Me"

CONTENTS

Chapter 1

GETTING STARTED

Freelancing can be big business if you follow a few simple steps to build a solid foundation. There has never been a better time to market yourself as a freelancer in the creative services field. With the web overcoming distance and travel, computers replacing drafting tables, and typesetters going the way of the Edsel, you can build a business based solely on education and experience.

1. Advantages to Self-Employment

For the first time in history, designers are free to create without specifying typefaces, counting characters, or waiting for type galleys. They can get client approvals from proofs available online. Writers are capable of pumping out turnkey newsletters with the help of software templates and distributing their publications online without spending a penny on printing or postage.

Once you master a knowledge of appropriate font usage and the elements of grid design, you'll be able to use your computer to generate a decent income. Finally, you really can have a profitable home-based business without stuffing envelopes — but only if you have an affinity for isolation. If you thrive on working alone and find that solitude recharges your batteries, you won't miss personal interaction. If you feel energized after flexing your interpersonal skills, you'll need to find outlets for them online, on the telephone, or at appointments.

If you thrive on working alone and find that solitude recharges your batteries, you won't miss personal interaction when freelancing.

In a recent survey, people with full-time jobs cited having a close friend in the workplace and a flexible schedule of prime importance. The same group responded that rank and title were more important than pay. These are easy job satisfactions to arrange when you're a freelancer. You decide your schedule, title, rank, and salary. Of course, the flip side of that equation is making enough money to pay your salary. I know one freelancer with a secret stash of business cards bearing the title "Supreme Lord and Master of the Universe." He says it helps when working with his more frustrating clients and reminds him of his power as a freelancer to walk away.

2. Launch Your Business Effectively

If you can't muster the small amount of capital required to invest in a computer, check out your local university or community college. Trade creative skills for computer time and work with the students on their school newspaper. Besides giving you some hands-on experience, this is a great opportunity to update your knowledge about what's hip in university life.

As an entrepreneur, you might qualify for a low-interest loan from the Small Business Administration (SBA) in the US. Application is simple if you follow the guidelines set out on their website, www.sba.gov, and fill out a few required forms. Depending on your location, you may even qualify for a HUBZone classification. (See Chapter 5 for more information about HUBZone classifications.) In Canada, Canada Business Service Centres, www.cbsc.org, provides information on sources of funding for small businesses, which vary from province to province/territory.

Once you get your equipment, the world is at your fingertips as long as you follow a few simple tips for building your freelance business. Don't get creative like one famous designer who started out in the in-house design department of a major corporation. About a year before he decided to launch his now legendary design studio, he started requisitioning computers, software, and furniture from his employer's purchasing department. These items were delivered to his new studio and were up and running the same day he submitted his resignation. He walked into his completely outfitted studio ready to hire five other designers. Few people knew the trick to how he made this smooth transition; most admire him and marvel at his business acumen.

3. Income Adventures and Other Paths

Unfortunately, most people who go into freelancing don't do so under ideal circumstances. More often, the ad agency you worked for lost a big account and had to cut back; or your salary was unjustifiable against billings. Sometimes you just annoy the wrong person. I worked at an animation studio and jumped when an art direction opportunity came along. The CEO interviewed me and fell in love with my leave-behind cartoon promotional piece. Unfortunately for me, the job he hired me for involved statistical publications: page after page of tabulations without a single cartoon in sight.

For the first six weeks I worked for him, all my employer talked about to his young wife was that cartoon and my amazing talent. She was standing next to him when he said he wanted me to decorate his new mansion because his wife had no taste. This was at a company cocktail party, and even if I could draw the expression on her face, you wouldn't believe it. From that day forward, she decided I was the enemy and hounded him to get rid of me. He couldn't tell me to my face that he was firing me or explain why; he instructed his CFO to do it. This genteel English gentleman walked into my office appearing quite overburdened. "I really don't know why, but I'm supposed to fire you," he said, looking puzzled.

Much earlier in my career, I worked at a downtown advertising agency and found myself working with an accomplished copywriter who turned out to be a great mentor for me. This creative director sported a Bette Davis pageboy hairstyle, smoked unfiltered Camels, and drove an old MG with the top down even though she was in her late forties. She lived with her gal pal in a big house in the suburbs.

One day, the owner of the company introduced me to a young man. "This is our new trainee and I expect you to show him the ropes." He had just graduated from the local state college. About a month later I was fired; they said my work wasn't up to snuff. The creative director pulled me aside and informed me the trainee was the son of the agency's largest client. My firing had nothing to do with the quality of my work. The new employee was receiving twice the salary for half the education and none of the experience. After this happens to you a few times, you start looking for alternative ways to earn a living. You, too, can decide to create a job outside the realm of office politics.

4. Find Your Professional Edge

No matter what you may have heard, talented people are drawn to other talented people by sheer magnetism. That inborn urge to raise standards pushes creatives above competitive mode. In the right environment, an encouraging, nurturing spirit takes hold of the principals, and true creatives revel in their compadres' success. If, in contrast, you find yourself mired in petty politics and devoting creative time to tripping up the other guy, you've lost your focus. If you're tired of playing games instead of creating great design or you've had it up to here with secretaries that think they have a better sense of type usage than you, then you are ready to freelance.

Maybe you just want to supplement your regular income. The reason doesn't matter. Nor does it matter what industry you work in now or where your experience lies. If you've got the motivation, you can succeed as a freelancer because people always need literature, websites, business cards, or whatever creative output you decide to sell. The challenge is how to attract them to your particular skill set, how to keep them coming back, and how to defend what's yours. There are some very specific things you can do to jump-start your business and start drawing in customers, and these are not limited to sending out little postcards by the thousands. Above all, don't follow in the footsteps of the famous designer I mentioned earlier. If you have a conscience, you'll spend most of your time looking over your shoulder, which will dilute the satisfaction of your success.

Even if you haven't established good discipline, there are certain characteristics that set professionals apart from amateurs. Read over this list and work on the areas you have not yet developed. Dust off and revisit the business skills you haven't used recently. As a freelancer, you represent yourself and are working for your own profit, not as an employee and not for the financial benefit of another person. If you were a clock-watcher or paced yourself on the job, get ready for a major restructuring of attitude.

4.1 Distinguish yourself from the competition

As a freelancer, you can provide value-added services to your clients. Perhaps you have a unique style of illustration or a working knowledge of local printers. Maybe you can offer an extensive type library and the know-how to use it, or a lengthy history of working in your client's industry. Whatever your skills, be prepared to describe them in detail. Distinguish yourself successfully, either through a unique promotion or ability, and you will stand out from the competition.

4.2   Showcase your abilities honestly

Your client will be greatly disappointed if you show him fantastic samples but he finds out later that you can't handle projects at that level. Do a little soul-searching before you construct your portfolio and make sure it truly represents the services you are qualified to sell. Remember, you'll be working by yourself and probably won't have anyone to hand off work to that you can't do. As you learn more and your work improves, add samples to your portfolio that reflect your full range of abilities.

4.3   Know your client's business

Before you make an appointment to see a new or potential client, do your homework. Learn as much as you can about the client's business and have a few compelling suggestions about how you can improve his creative work. Focus on how your skills add value, and offer solutions not previously tried. For instance, suggest the use of humor or concept development that stresses soft sell rather than hard sell. If you have examples of work designed for the same industry or service as your client's, make sure you include them in your portfolio. Previous experience in the same area relieves some of a potential client's anxiety about your familiarity with his business or industry.

4.4   Strive to build long-term relationships

Bring all the same virtues you would to friendship, but don't expect your client to reciprocate until the benefits you provide are realized and trust is established. Trust is built over time, so if you have a prospect who hasn't approached you with a job, take him out to lunch. People want to know they share a similar set of values before they will trust you with their work.

4.5   Share your resourcefulness and problem-solving skills

Provide specific examples of how you might handle a creative problem. Offer solutions and detail how you rescued a previous project.

Focus on how your skills add value, and offer solutions not previously tried.

However, be careful about making suggestions for improvements to your client's previous design pieces. You never know how much the client had to do with the design, and you might end up insulting his taste. Keep your opinions about someone else's work to yourself, because they may create hard feelings and subtract from the trust you're trying to build with your new client.

4.6 Stay in close contact during a project

Remember that your client has an active interest in his project. Understand that providing timely information is imperative when a decision needs to be made that affects price or delivery of the finished job. Resist the urge to give the go-ahead without your client's approval, no matter how much pressure you are under.

Resist the urge to give the go-ahead without your client's approval, no matter how much pressure you are under.

4.7 Treat everyone respectfully

You may only work with the owner, but everyone in the office plays a part in building a business. You never know who will be responsible for projects in the future. Keep in mind that employees share opinions and experiences; make sure all their experiences with you are positive.

4.8 Join professional organizations

Find your local chapter of the Art Directors' Club, the Production Managers' Association, or a local group of professional photographers. Listen and learn. Make friends with your peers and share your experience, even if it's limited. Nobody will understand your problems better than someone in the same business. Most accomplished professionals are eager to help people just starting out and carry a wealth of experience they won't mind sharing.

4.9 Keep boasting to yourself

Your client will be able to see your skill by the specific work samples in your portfolio. Paying unnecessary lip service to your range of talent is overkill. Before you know it, like Narcissus, you'll drown in a pool of your own making. Express all your self-adulation in front of the mirror, where it will boost self-confidence you might lose later while making cold calls.

4.10 Sell clients only what they need

Develop a good understanding of your clients' budget requirements and the competition in their industry, then select the services and products that provide the best fit. Your clients will appreciate your efforts and see through any featherbedding. Always practice the Golden Rule: *Do unto others as you would have them do unto you.*

4.11 Remember, it's the little things

If you're interested in building credibility, keep your promises. Call back when you say you will, meet your deadlines, stick to delivery schedules, and stay within budget even if it costs you. Jobs are only awarded after trust has been established. A missed deadline is all it takes to shake a client's trust in your ability.

4.12 Be businesslike in all your dealings

Whether you work with the boss's secretary or have access to the chief executive officer, don't drop in unannounced or overstay your welcome. Make sure you only call your client when you really need to. Access to the key decision-maker is easily lost if you abuse your privilege.

Achieving success as a freelancer is easy if you put your mind to it. Computer technology has changed many fields, and you will be required to handle massive amounts of information. For instance, technology makes it possible for you to not only design but also do some data entry, check facts, and do your own proofreading. The scope of services you offer must be greater than ever before.

Turnkey jobs bring in more money because the more work you can do yourself, the more money you can make. How well you manage various aspects of a project will determine your success. As your relationships with your clients grow, clients will rely on you as their communication beacon and will expect more from you than they might have just a few months ago. You must be dependable and progressive, and you must maintain an active interest in your clients' successes.

Create a sense of ease when doing business and provide cost-saving tips whenever possible. Get up to date on paper stock, trends

in ink and varnish applications, or the latest industry catchphrases. (See the CD included with this book for a list of resources.) Present copy and design solutions that overshadow both your competition and the client's competition. Give sound advice gleaned from your own experience as well as the experiences shared by your peers at professional meetings. There are many mediocre designers. Once a client finds a reliable creative source with the right expertise and problem-solving ability, he or she will usually cling to you. But first you must earn his or her trust.

If you thrive on working alone and find that solitude recharges your batteries, you won't miss personal interaction.

Chapter 2

CREATING YOUR WORK ENVIRONMENT

Starting your own business gives you many freedoms. Of course, each freedom comes with a matching responsibility. One of the most important responsibilities is to yourself — to create a work environment conducive to producing excellent output. Freelancers have to adjust to complete and total freedom while turning out excellent work in a timely manner. You'll need to minimize distractions, organize your time, and create a routine that defines the limits of your freedom if you want to make a good living — which is the reward for creating a work environment that supports a strong work ethic.

First, set some boundaries regarding your time and space, then explain them carefully to your family (including the kids) and friends. Even if you live in a 25-room mansion, establishing boundaries right from the start will make things easier as your business grows.

Your perfect work space largely depends on the type of creative service you provide, money available to invest, and your personal preference. One freelance writer set up her home office after her cushy executive position with a major corporation evaporated. She certainly never missed her daily two-hour commute, but she couldn't shake the feeling of being unemployed. After some serious soul-searching, she realized her need for a clear time delineation between work and home. She discovered that even a short drive to a different location supplied that separation; eventually she abandoned her home office for the well-defined structure of a rented office suite. She had a place to go, a sense of employment, and a professional office in which to meet clients. "'Know yourself' is my best advice to newbiz-bees," she said, free advice from a 25-year marketing professional who couldn't live without that commute.

1. Pros and Cons of a Portable Desktop

For writers, a reliable laptop that goes with you everywhere may suffice, especially if money is an issue. This is cutting-edge operations management and deserves applause, if for nothing more than saving a few trees. It's also a great way to give top-notch presentations either to promote your business or to pitch an idea for a project. When you carry your business in a laptop, even the public library provides an instant office. Meetings with clients become easier, checking on project status is a phone jack or wireless connection away, and finishing off that last paragraph can be accomplished during a ride on the subway.

Of course, if you take your eyes off that precious cargo, a thief may make off with your life's work and that's the end of you. For your own peace of mind and protection, make sure you've made backup disks for all your software and everything on your computer, especially your current projects. Make SOS stand for *Safe or Sorry* rather than the more colloquial *Save Often, Stupid*. Additionally, a replacement value insurance policy for your computer (just in case) may be a worthwhile investment. The insurance industry will gladly accommodate you, and a quick replacement is then just a phone call away.

Not all creative pursuits are so easily accommodated, and your business may not flourish within the restrictions of a laptop computer. Buying a second system as backup is an excellent idea, both for safety's sake and networking capability. "Heavy-duty desktop systems are comparatively cheap and light-duty laptops are dropping in price, so I store all working documents on my laptop so I can grab it and run," says Brian Dooley, a well-established technical writer in New Zealand. "This keeps my work within arm's reach no matter where I'm at." You may also have to prepare slick comprehensives for client review, collate multipage publications, and execute other precise activities that require natural light plus a stable, clean work area. The laptop office will not suffice for these extra endeavors.

2. Set Up an Efficient Home Office

If you think you need more than a cyber office or fall into the "other creative endeavor" category, here are a few tips to keep in mind when setting up your home office.

2.1 Dedicate your work space

If you live alone, you can turn your entire living space into your office, though this is not recommended, for obvious reasons. Most people have family, pets, and surprise visitors to consider when they work at home, not to mention the need to tidy up before a client appears. The ideal home office is a dedicated room with a door that locks. Why would you need a lock in your own home? The first time Junior accidentally deletes work to make room on your hard drive for his new computer game, the reason will become eminently clear. When your spouse needs poster board for a yard sale sign, locking the door will protect your five-dollar-a-sheet, double-weight, plate illustration board in your absence. Plus, the expensive photo-quality laser jet paper you bought to print out your client's color comprehensives will not be reallocated without your knowledge for the family reunion snapshots.

To produce like a professional, your work space must be pared down to provide the necessary accoutrements for peak performance.

For a truly dedicated work space, remove all items not related to your work. First, you don't want to allow your office to become a pseudo storage space packed with clutter. If you're going to produce like a professional, your work space must be pared down to provide the necessary accoutrements for peak performance. That means no distractions like that old black-and-white TV you've held onto since your college days. Give it to charity and take a tax deduction for the donation.

Second, the tax department (aka the Internal Revenue Service or Canada Revenue Agency) will not allow you to write off a percentage of your monthly expenses on your income tax return if the space you call your office is also used as the laundry room or Little League equipment locker. It must be a *dedicated space*.

Spend a few dollars on proper cable clamps and arrange all the electrical cables, computer connections, and surge protectors so they don't interfere with your movement. (You do have surge protectors on your equipment to protect your investment, don't you?) Be prepared for the unexpected: My new computer arrived and I was ready to work when curiosity almost killed the cat. Up he jumped, ever so gracefully knocking over a large glass of iced tea — right

There's no greater challenge to turning out good work than an uncomfortable chair.

into the keyboard. No work for me that day. My new keyboard arrived the next day, and you can bet the cat was outdoors. I had learned the importance of a dedicated work space.

2.2 Create a work-friendly ambiance

The key to getting down to work is creating a work-friendly environment that will disappear into the background so you can concentrate on the project at hand. This includes excellent lighting. If you deal with colors, you will need both a yellow and a white bulb to mimic natural light. There's a reason those green peppers look so very green in the grocery store, and you need to believe what you see when suggesting colors to clients. Poor lighting contributes to eye strain, and most creativity involves the use of vision, so take care. Direct your excellent lighting at the thing that needs illuminating, not at your eyes.

Odors and stale air can be just as much of a distraction as the neighbor's kid bouncing a ball off the side of your house, so plug in a few scent generators (or remove the ones your well-meaning spouse plugged in if scents are a distraction for you).

Temperature is important, too, so a portable fan or small heater may offer comfort, depending on the season. You won't be able to concentrate if your feet are cold. When you achieve homeostasis and your surroundings fade from your attention, your focus will be on your work, allowing your creativity and productivity to soar.

2.3 Invest in a great chair

If you spend 30 percent of your time seated in front of a computer, you certainly deserve an ergonomically correct chair that will support you during the long haul and late-night pushes to meet contract deadlines. If you need to convince yourself to invest the money, remember that it's tax deductible, and if you spread out the expenditure over a couple of projects, you'll find a good chair is not that expensive after all.

There's no greater challenge to turning out good work than an uncomfortable chair. Spending $1,000 on a well-designed chair pays off over time with fewer interruptions due to a stiff back and fewer painful distractions from the real reason you're sitting there in the first place. Keep in mind that buying a chair is like buying a new mattress. You should sit in it before you buy it. My personal favorite is the Aeron Chair by Herman Miller. There are many chair designers in the marketplace, and the advent of online shopping provides some great deals on fine furniture that otherwise might prove cost-prohibitive. Go on, you deserve it. Think of it as an investment in your "well seated" success.

2.4 Buy a good computer

Whether you work on a laptop or prefer a massive tower and 22-inch monitor, remember you get what you pay for. Spend some time talking to other people in your field. Ask them why they chose their computer; how much downtime they've had due to hardware problems; how easy it was to get the equipment fixed when there was a problem; and if they ever used a backup system. Remember that running your own business involves taking care of your own problems. Your client will not care about why you missed his million-dollar deadline; he will only remember that you did. There are no excuses or second chances when you cost your client money.

Buying the best equipment you can afford will save you a lot of potential grief. Like others, you may be afraid of buying equipment that will be out of date before it's paid for. This is a common problem when technology moves as fast as it does today. Leasing is an excellent option for the short term. Just make sure you read the small print on the lease agreement.

If you're working by yourself and on a limited budget, look for reliability. In this regard, you can't beat Macintosh. Contrary to popular myth, there are more than 3 million Apple users who swear by their machines, and I'm one of them. Information technology departments all over the country saved a few hundred dollars on corporate PC purchases but spent millions creating the technical-support teams required to keep their hardware up and running. Now that prices of the two operating systems are almost the same, it makes good sense to buy the one that's the least time-consuming and troublesome to maintain. If you want to be self-sufficient, my advice is to buy a Mac.

A few words about your Graphical User Interface (GUI): It was great news for PC owners when Windows was introduced, but it's just a big piece of software that reproduces the inherent graphic interface of the Mac's operating system. Windows takes longer to react to commands and requires more keystrokes, plus it takes up valuable drive space. None of this matters if you have the capital to fund an IT department to install new software for you, work out bugs, and cater to all your hardware needs. If you want to be self-reliant, though, buy reliable equipment — buy a Mac.

Macs are designed for people who use computers in their work but don't want to spend time working *on* their computers. Finding software is no problem, either, especially if you shop at any one of the dedicated Macintosh sites such as MacConnection or Mac Warehouse. (Check the CD for more information.)

Another advantage to buying Macintosh is rarely mentioned yet is of particular interest to the creative professional. The graphic interface is more intuitive. This means there is less shifting from the left (logic) side of the brain to the right (emotion) side, and as most creative people know, the longer you remain in touch with your emotional side, the better your creative output. Macintosh allows you to spend more time concentrating on creative output and less time figuring out how to get your computer to do what you want. The best value on the market right now is the iMac. At the time of writing, for less than $800 USD, you can get an iMac with a G4 processor, an internal modem, a CD-ROM reader, a full-color screen, a keyboard, and a mouse. All you need to do is plug it in and turn it on. The savings in trips to the repair shop make it ideal for someone just starting out.

2.5 Own the right equipment for the job

Do you have the right equipment to finish the jobs you compete for in the marketplace? Again, think turnkey: the more you can do to push the job to completion, the more money you get to keep. And back up jobs properly. Computer hard drives are getting bigger and faster every day, and it's tempting to store everything on your computer and neglect having an archive system for completed jobs. The first time you can't retrieve a file or find a piece of art, you will realize the importance of having a backup copy. As a regular part of client service, supply a copy of the completed project on CD-ROM for the customer's archive, and inform her or him that you maintain a backup copy as insurance. This is a value-added, no-cost bonus for any client and builds high rate-of-return for customers.

Basic equipment for your home office should include all the necessary peripherals required to complete a job. When providing hard copies, you will need a high-end, photo-quality color laser jet printer such as those made by Epson. A flatbed scanner with OCR (optical character recognition) capability is another important piece of equipment: it will avoid a lot of data entry. Pay close attention, though, because this software is still not perfected.

For transferring files and archiving, buy a good-quality DVD/CD burner. Forget about floppy disks, 3.5-inch disks, and Zip disks; nobody uses them anymore because of their low storage capacity and the high risk of transferring a virus. Blank CDs are a dollar a dozen and can hold ten times what a Zip disk holds — plus they create a permanent record. For archiving, CDs and DVDs can be sleeved and stored in a three-ring binder, minimizing storage space. Shop online for the best deals in equipment and storage media, including the sleeves or jewel cases to package your archival CDs. Online is also a good place to locate deals on blank CDs and DVDs. Computer catalogs frequently use media storage as a loss leader, sold at cost to attract customers.

2.6 Upgrade your software frequently

Each industry has a set of tried-and-true software packages that have proven instrumental in bringing some very old trades into the digital age. If you are a writer, your favorite data processing program may be Microsoft Word. But if you branch out into scripts, you will need a scripting package to cut down on the drudgery of sticking to proper form. As a designer, you will need a software package that complements the requirements of your suppliers. (Although some suppliers are limited in the software they have on hand, most stock an assortment of packages just so they can output whatever files they receive.)

A word of caution: The type of software you use can easily tag your level of proficiency in the industry. For instance, a designer who prepares layouts in Corel Draw will reveal his status as an amateur. As one industry insider remarked: "Fixing the mistakes of naive designers is a big problem for prepress professionals. A lot of time is lost in prepress as we arm-wrestle files into something useful. This week, maybe 10 percent of the files are a nuisance. Next week, it could be 60 percent of the files. It's pretty unpredictable in this business, but the market is so soft, you really can't say no to the work." (For more on this problem, see Chapter 4.)

Using out-of-date or inefficient software tells everybody you're behind the times in prepress know-how; some programs are just not designed to handle the high-end requirements of today's digital print equipment. And once your job causes trouble on the press, the print shop will label you as a time-consuming client. As my adver-

The type of software you use can easily tag your level of proficiency in the industry.

Some programs are just not designed to handle the high-end requirements of today's digital print equipment.

tising professor at the Columbus College of Art and Design, Jeff Link, admonished me: "Snap out of it, kid. If you want to do this, do what's necessary, whatever is necessary. Do it right or make room for someone who will." That was *my* reality check.

2.6a Know the difference between programs

QuarkXPress is preferred in some advertising agencies and design studios. However, many designers have switched from what they call "Quirk" to the Adobe software InDesign. InDesign evolved from PageMaker and has proven over time to be more stable in larger publications and are particularly good at converting documents to PDF (Portable Document Format), the file format used worldwide for all kinds of output.

You must choose the software you feel most comfortable using. It makes no sense to buy software that inhibits your ability to produce quality work. Many designers have abandoned QuarkXPress for InDesign simply because Adobe is a larger, more stable company, one that they feel confident will be around to issue updates, provide user support, and satisfy customer demand. Remember that PostScript, a data-transfer file type developed by Adobe, is inherent in all Adobe software, but is not native to Quark, which can lead to problems with Quark PDF files. Just ask any printer whose prepress technician has stayed up all night to get their level 3 PostScript software to output the client's level 1A PostScript Quark file.

Since Quark is not a PDF native or quartz-based application, it has to fall back on QuickDraw to render the contents of the *save as PDF output*. QuickDraw can't capture the incredible detail of PostScript, so Quark makes some internal transformations of its PostScript file. This is most likely the reason users complain of color and resolution shifts. It's called color-space shifting and refers to the PostScript Printer Description (PPD) used to create the PDF. Sometimes Quark will take an existing PDF and misread the CMYK color space. One industry insider quipped: "Quark is trying to reinvent itself as a developer of work-flow management tools. If it can't sort out problems like this one soon, it won't have any work to flow."

There are two levels of PDF in use today. The X-1A standard used by Quark is more restrictive, based on a limited set of acceptable color spaces (CMYK and spot). The more advanced X-3 standard allows for other color spaces such as RGB, provided they are appropriately tagged with ICC profiles. This is all handled automatically if you are using Adobe software and don't check the box titled

"Convert CMYK to RGB" when using Distiller. I've even heard that using Color Management (CMS) causes PostScript output to read CMYK as RGB. Turn it off before you export as PDF and avoid output problems.

2.6b Choose software that suits the work you do

If you design complex, layered, single-sheet brochures, you may still prefer QuarkXPress. But if you want a no-nonsense layout program for bread-and-butter work such as software manuals, use InDesign. Adobe has incorporated many of the features that made Quark attractive to designers when it first hit the market, and there's not much difference in capability anymore. Keep in mind that if your favorite print shop only accepts files created in PageMaker, compatibility may make it profitable in the long run to switch. There is a converter that works between the two programs, but much like OCR, you may still have to rework the end result so it matches the original, particularly text blocks, which don't convert well. If you want to rely on a converter, plan on spending money for last-minute corrections. It would be great if all software programs worked for all job requirements, but that's not the case. You will create a more stable document if you import graphics created in a program designed for specific functions as opposed to doing the calisthenics of making something like Microsoft Word do what it wasn't designed to do.

My preference is Adobe Freehand MX because it is an excellent alternative to Adobe Illustrator when creating logos and pdfs. Freehand has stability and conversion capability when it comes to creating Encapsulated PostScript (eps) files for placement in layout programs. Freehand also allows you to save your documents in more than ten different formats, including several compatible versions of Illustrator files, Photoshop files, PDF, GIF, JPEG, and Flash. Your best bet is to choose Adobe Creative Suite and you'll have everything you need.

2.7 Establish good work habits

Decide if you want to treat your work as a hobby or pursue business with the intent of building either a steady income or a major conglomerate. This decision will help you structure your day. If you like to get up around noon and enjoy life, you may need a loving, fully employed spouse to generate income that pays the bills. Being self-employed requires strict discipline when it comes to establishing regular operating hours, being accessible to your clients, managing time to accommodate finding new business, and finishing up the paperwork necessary for billing and payables. After you do all that, don't forget to make time for the actual creative work. And you thought self-employment meant unfettered creative pursuit. It does; just think of it as creative multitasking.

Choose your work hours, knowing you have the freedom to extend or delay them as deadlines loom or family vacations take center stage. This is the true freedom of running a business, and you can manage it if you don't abuse it. Don't wait for your bank account to dictate when to get back to work. Let your clients know when they can reach you as well as when they can't. Set firm boundaries on this issue if you must. If you have a client who persists in calling you at all hours of the night just to touch base, put your foot down, but do it politely. Freelancing shouldn't mean you become a slave to the telephone. Tell your family when your time is off limits and make sure the boundary is clear. If there is no current project, don't go off for a week's worth of golf. Spend at least part of your time cultivating new business. You'll feel much better about time spent looking for your next job than you will about perfecting your swing (and guilt will always yield a YIP!). Of course it's more fun to curl up with a bowl of popcorn in the middle of the afternoon and watch a Cubs game, but that won't make the car payments. Have a plan and stick to it. You'll reap the rewards of good work habits: an abundant project list, loyal clients, and a healthy bank balance.

2.8 Upgrade phone lines and Internet access

Depending on your location, the type of Internet access you use, and whether there are teenagers in your house, installing an extra phone line with a dedicated phone number might be required. If you use a dial-up connection for your online work, an extra phone line may be a *necessity*. Don't be embarrassed about having dial-up instead of broadband. There are 48 million dial-up users in the USA alone. The only drawback is that some online features (like video) will not be accessible. If an extra line for the dial-up is beyond your budget, an easy, low-cost alternative is using digital voice mail provided by most local phone companies to handle incoming calls while you work online. Your calls will be answered before they ever reach your phone, sparing clients a constant busy signal.

If you have online access via a cable modem, wireless T1 or T2 broadband, consider getting rid of your phone line altogether and using an online provider such as Vonage. (See the CD for details.) They supply an adapter box that connects to your modem interface. Plug your phones in and start dialing. You can realize incredible savings by eliminating your phone and long-distance carrier and opting for cable phone service. Current offers include a $40 credit for customers who make referrals plus the same amount in credit for the new customer. The most popular plan in the US offers unlimited nationwide calls and 500 minutes of international long distance for a flat monthly rate that is less than you pay for local service.

Keep in mind that your cable broadband must be at least 500k to prevent signal falloff, when your party's voice trails off into the void. If you don't mind a few empty, extended pauses, try it on your 256k modem. Most of these services will allow you to keep your local phone number or even create a new number with your choice of area code (as long as it is not taken by somebody else). With the advent of deregulation, satellite phone and cable companies are offering lucrative package deals bundling phone, Internet, and television services for a set fee. Keep in mind some companies require a contract while others do not. In the US, visit www.bundlemyservices.com to look for deals.

If you never want to miss a call, a mobile phone is the obvious answer. One scriptwriter I know sleeps, eats, and showers with her cell phone within arm's reach. Having a cell phone also solves the dilemma of nonbusiness calls competing for telephone time. It's easy to restrict the use of your cell phone to business calls by only giving the number to clients.

What about facsimiles? Most people use email to send documents these days, but if you deal with clients who are reticent to enter the digital age, you may be required to have a working fax machine. If so, a dedicated line may be the best choice for ease of operation and rapid exchange of hard copies. Let your volume of work determine need.

Choose your Internet service provider (ISP) according to the type of creative work you do online. If you send large files for output in this worldwide market, broadband is definitely worth the expense. Different areas have different services available. There are many options even in rural areas, and the selection is growing.

Choose your Internet service provider (ISP) according to the type of creative work you do online.

Whether you choose satellite dish access, cable modem access, wireless access, DSL, ISDN, T1 or T2, or dial-up, make sure you choose a reliable server and an ISP that meets the demands of your business. (See the CD included with this book for further information about choosing an ISP.)

Most service providers experience some glitches as they struggle to keep up with and work out the bugs in the latest technology. That said, don't let a bad choice make you miserable. Ask professional peers what providers they prefer and be prepared to change yours if it's less than satisfactory.

If your means of Internet access (e.g., cable) requires a special modem, make sure you shop for it online. My local cable company charges $129.99 for a modem I found online through Yahoo! Shopping for $34. Checking sources online is well worth your time. Another good source is Buy.com, especially for wireless routers.

2.9 Create a business image

Creating a dedicated work space includes creating a professional image. Even in today's digital era, you will need a business card and some form of stationery, either as a workable template that you can print as needed or a professionally designed letterhead package printed by an old-fashioned letterpress printer. You will also find it useful to have a JPEG image of your business card to include with email correspondence. Remember one of the keys to creating a successful image: *act as if*.

If you are capable of competing with industry leaders, make sure your image shows it. Looking for serious work requires a serious image appropriate to industry expectations. If you want to be a clown, make your business card colorful and fun, with a wild and crazy typeface. Otherwise, use good sense when selecting your identity font; choose something well-proven that doesn't shout, "I'm an amateur."

Creative counsel requires cutting-edge imagination, yet nothing detracts more than the latest-fad fonts. If in doubt, consult a professional designer. However, don't let all this conservatism *inhibit* your creativity. The creative services field allows more leeway than other business arenas when it comes to self-promotion. My advice is to rein in your wildly creative side just a tad so you don't frighten the average businessperson. If you scare them, or suggest you are completely uncontrollable, they won't hire you.

An important aspect frequently overlooked by the overzealous marketer is clarity: Can you read the phone number or do you need a magnifying glass and a translator to figure out what it says? Can you only read it because you know what it's supposed to say? Your client won't know what it says and won't be able to reach you because of it.

Remember the purpose of your business card. It was from the lowly calling card that the business card evolved; it gives the recipient an impression, one carefully controlled by design and stock selection. (Victorian society first had social cards featuring only a name, then calling cards, then the business card evolved.) Subtle details create the desired impression, so tread carefully.

Steer clear of flashy thermography, which is a cheap substitute for engraving. Would you cover your Jaguar's dash with pink shag carpeting? Wear climbing boots with a Yves St. Laurent strapless gown? Probably not. Thermography has the same effect for those who know the difference between true engraving and expanded plastic powder sprinkled on ink to raise the type.

Another thing to avoid at all costs is handing out your business card for personal purposes; this will dilute its effect and render you quickly cardless. It's bad form to hand out business cards in a bar; use your business card to get business, your personal card to get dates.

Keep in mind the code of card turning. The code was originally intended for social cards. As Judith Martin explains in *Miss Manners' Guide to Excruciatingly Correct Behavior*, such cards "are hardly used now that people imagine they have better things to do with their time than to ride about in their carriages all morning, paying calls on one another. So you may amaze and delight your business acquaintances, as well as mystify them, by turning cards on them." She continues: "There are four statements you can make just by bending your business card's corners. They are: *visité* (upper left), meaning you have appeared with the card in person; *félicitation* (upper right), meaning that you congratulate the recipient; *congé* (lower left), which announces that you are leaving town; and *condolence* (lower right), which is, of course, an expression of sympathy. If you promise to revive this custom, Miss Manners will permit you to get funny with it by, say, turning both bottom corners for 'Too bad, I'm leaving you' or both right corners for 'Congratulations on your loss.'"*

* Judith Martin, *Miss Manners' Guide to Excruciatingly Correct Behavior*. (New York: Warner Books, 1983), 509.

Lay a good foundation when you create your work space, and both your creativity and client list will grow.

Let's dig up a truly overused cliché: You reap what you sow. Starting a business is like starting a garden. Setting up your work environment is like using a plow and fertilizer to condition the soil. Seed (cover the town with promotional material), feed (reconfirm and recontact until you become a familiar face), and weed it (head off the competition) until your garden is lush and reaps a bounty of rewards. Leave it untended, ignore your clients, and pretty soon some nasty weeds will take over. Lay a good foundation when you create your work space, and both your creativity and client list will grow.

3. Supplying Your Own Employee Benefits

Health Insurance for Freelancers

My worst nightmare became reality when I hurt my back. I had been freelancing for about three years, but still hadn't accumulated enough regular work to buy health insurance. Besides, I had jobs with design studios and small companies at various times during my career that didn't provide employee benefits, so it wasn't something I missed. It's a common occurrence in the commercial art industry; margins are so tight, many employers simply cannot meet the rent, pay the salaries, and offer a competitive benefit package. Freelance teaches you a deep appreciation for employee benefits, but perhaps not enough to give up freedom (yes, put on your best Mel Gibson blue face, thank you).

A client, who also happened to be a nurse, took pity on me; actually, I think she was more interested in getting her projects completed. She got me in to see a well known back doctor who examined my films. "Yes, I think I can help you ... in fact, I can relieve that pain in less than five minutes, but not today. You come and see me when you have health insurance." He patted me on the back as he pushed me out of his office, bent over, limping, tears in my eyes from the pain shooting down my right leg to my toes.

Eventually, I went to the public hospital and waited for more than 12 hours to see a doctor. During that time, an orderly demanded my gurney because he needed it for a more serious injury until I promised to lie on the floor if he took it.

If you can spare yourself the economic inequities of not getting proper health care, here are some important tips about finding employee benefits for yourself. If worst comes to worst and you don't have enough regular work to support a health plan, free clinics still exist. You can find a free clinic in your area here: http://find-ahealthcenter.hrsa.gov by typing in your address. In most cases, clinics are free or charge a small fee, sometimes on a sliding scale. You may not get the help you need, but chances are they will be able to refer you to someone who can help. Community-based organizations have vast connections in all areas of human need. Don't be proud.

First, decide what's most important to you. If you want to keep costs low and are relatively young and healthy, choose coverage with a low monthly payment and a high deductible. Or just buy major medical; you'll want just enough to cover you in case of emergencies. If you want a plan that reduces the cost of doctor's visits, prescriptions, and has a low deductible, don't be shocked at the cost. You will get more complete coverage with a stable company like Humana who also offer codicils (little amendments they attach to bigger things like vision and dental). That can be a handy thing if you have a sweet tooth like me.

Here are a few places to start looking; take some time to sit down and appraise your needs, your family's needs and existing conditions or potential hereditary diseases. Remember that prices are limited by legislation, so determining factors like deductibles and coverage limits will be key to finding a monthly payment you can live with. A good thing is that all health care costs are 100 percent deductible on your income taxes, so it's not all bad. Verify this information here: http://www.irs.gov/businesses/article/0,,id=181005,00.HTML.

You don't have to make any more bad investments to have a decent tax write-off (you fat cat, you). Remember, if the monthly cost is too good to be true, you've either got a super high deductible or the coverage is extremely limited. Pay close attention to what's covered and what's not; especially pre-existing conditions or stuff hidden in your genes. You might not have it yet, but if Mom and Dad both had it, chances are good that it's in your future, too.

A few ways to keep costs down:

- If you don't go to the doctor more than once a year, consider carrying only major medical for emergencies.

- Check with design trade and professional associations to see if they have a group plan. Even joining a group like the National Business Association of America will help provide group rates around $500 per month for a family of four with $10 co-pays. Rates will be lower and coverage will be guaranteed on pre-existing conditions if you are part of a group. Now here's something an AIGA membership should offer our community, but doesn't.

- Shop online. Insurance companies pay fewer broker fees when you deal direct.

- Find out if you're eligible to use a medical savings account (MSA).

The US Health Insurance Portability and Accountability Act (HIPAA) makes certain allowances for the self-employed. This lets you enjoy benefits from a higher deductible insurance policy (with reduced premiums) and use pre-tax dollars to pay for expenses up to your deductible limit.

If you can't find health insurance in the US because of a pre-existing condition, the HIPAA may help you obtain it. This site will help you find out if you live in one of 34 states who have some form of risk pool: http://www.healthinsurance.org/risk_pools. You can also find additional information here: http://www.selfemployedcountry.org/main.HTML

It's pretty hard to find a deal, but I've located some good places to start looking.

- https://www.mostchoice.com/health-insurance.cfm
- https://www.insureme.com
- http://www.insurancevalues.com
- https://www.ehealthinsurance.com
- http://www.alliedquotes.com
- http://www.healthinsurancefinders.com

If worst comes to worst and you find yourself in a hospital emergency room without insurance, remember (even if they don't) that you are a human being and have a right to your dignity. Spit back if necessary, but don't give up your gurney.

Chapter 3

TAKE A PERSONAL AND PORTFOLIO INVENTORY

The marketplace for creative services is like a big fishbowl. There's only so much food in the bowl and everybody has to eat. You will be competing with some pretty big fish, so take a careful look at your experience and the competition before you decide who to tackle.

For various reasons, clients in the bank business like to see samples of bank brochures while clients in the grocery business want to see food brochures. This stems from the perception that their industry is particular and requires a sensitive eye. It can be hard to communicate to these clients that design is the careful manipulation of white space, whether you're moving copy that supports pictures of suits at a conference table or pickles in a jar. Even fewer clients realize the real art in scripting a phrase that moves an unwilling purchaser or grabs the attention of a customer for their product or service.

Will you be the right freelancer to handle the challenges and tight cornering at high speeds required by this client? Depending on how fluid you can be in adapting to clients' needs, you might be. One ad campaign I developed for an emerging medical products manufacturer said just that, "We adjust to our customer's needs like water adjusts to the shape of its container." If you can communicate this attitude when you meet a potential client, you've just discovered one of the secrets of landing the job. As a freelance designer,

I have designed ads for unusual products such as bull semen, everyday items such as washers and dryers, a calendar for an architectural firm, a very different kind of calendar for the ladies' club Chippendales, and a myriad of conservative corporate publications. I've done editorial illustrations, margin cartoons in a reference book, and a series of full-color ads for a couple of skyscrapers just to name a few. One thing for sure: I've never been bored. If you enjoy variety, you will be limited only by your fears and unwillingness to reach out. If you have the courage, an endless variety of projects await you.

1. Know Your Skills and Resources

Although opportunities to exercise your creativity are limitless, the flip side is that everybody in this business says they can do it all, especially printers. They don't want to be left out of the game, but unless they plan to refer the work to someone who *can* do it, or subcontract the work out, they are stepping into the black hole of unfulfilled promises. If you say you can produce a particular piece when you know there's no way, you may just find *yourself* accountable when the project fails. Remember, a client with a bad experience is a client who won't call again.

Here's a story about one time I quite naively overstepped my own know-how. When I was still in art school, I accepted an illustration job for a small ad agency. The assignment was to create a pen-and-ink drawing of a man's hand holding a hammer. How hard could that be? But when I was in high school, boys took "shop" (woodworking or mechanics) and girls took home economics, which didn't cover the proper way to hold a hammer. After I dropped off the finished art I got an angry call from the art director — and justifiably so. He couldn't use my perfectly executed illustration on a business card for his client, a professional carpenter, "unless the latest thing is holding a hammer like a spatula."

As this story shows, it pays to do a little research before you start a job. Even before you start freelancing, sit down and carefully examine your experience and capabilities. What is your education? Does your experience in the field fill in for the gaps in your formal education? Have you mastered communication skills that allow you to present your work in a professional manner, or would it be smarter for you to market yourself in places that don't require personal presentations? Decide on your strengths *and* your limitations before you promote yourself to other people for hire.

> If you have the courage, an endless variety of projects await you.

Managers and owners who rely on your skills are putting their reputations on the line. If you sell yourself as something you're not, you risk your reputation *and theirs* if you fail to deliver. Before you start marketing your skills, take time to make a detailed evaluation of exactly what those skills are. Have a clear picture of your abilities and build the promotion of your skills from the hard facts. If you frequently use hyperbole or slide into "creative writing" rather easily, it might be prudent to ask one of your professional peers to do an objective evaluation of your skills.

Honest representation of your skills will reveal your integrity and keep you out of trouble, as the following story illustrates. As the art director on an annual report for a major client, I knew all the tricks we employed for a particular photo shoot. The truth is, we had to invent a few new tricks to corral the subject of the shoot, protective gear. Made out of rubber, it just wouldn't stay put, bouncing around every time someone took a breath. I had to use all kinds of tape and florist's goop to get the rubber bits to stay in place long enough for the photographer to work.

I showed this annual report to a prospective client and was asked some very pointed questions about it. I was puzzled by her intense curiosity about this particular piece. She explained, "Another person was just in here with this in his portfolio, but he couldn't answer any of my technical questions, whereas you have." It turns out a production trainee from the print shop handling the job was also pitching the client and grabbed a few finished pieces from his company's sample drawer. Unfortunately, he had only been a trainee for a month and knew very little about actual production and nothing about art direction. By all means aspire to greatness, but don't mislead people unless you have an extra $50,000 to reprint a botched job. And don't ever sink to showing someone else's work as your own.

2. Welcome Variety and Challenge the Competition

Now that you know what you can do, what do you enjoy? Remember all those times when the good jobs went to your superiors and you got the leftovers? Freelancing lets you pick and choose the type of assignment you want in good times. In bad times, when the pickings are slim, you'll be surprised how much you enjoy putting together a car parts catalog. There's no joy in not being able to make the mortgage payment, but it's easy to enjoy thinking of ways to spend your profit while you move little pieces of line art to match the right copy block.

Bread-and-butter work is not exciting or glamorous — it doesn't give you an opportunity to try out all those cool effects in Photoshop. When the posh stuff with the unlimited budget that makes a splashy portfolio piece comes along, make the most of it. Keep in mind that every job that crosses your desktop won't be a portfolio piece. Don't stick up your nose at drudge work, because the money spends the same, and as a freelancer, the object is to make money. This is only one of the ways things have changed since you became self-employed.

We would all like to spend our time designing beautiful things, but remember the fishbowl? The general rule is the big fish go after the big jobs. You will find yourself competing with some pretty big fish for the better work and, in hard times, even for small contracts. (I discuss how to protect your business and maintain control of jobs in Chapter 4.) Don't be intimidated if you find yourself competing against a big studio. You may know their reputation, but a reputation may be the result of something completely different than raw talent and ability, as the following story illustrates.

One designer I met while freelancing worked at the number one design studio in a major metropolitan area. This studio was considered primo, and everybody wanted to work in their 40th-floor atrium office uptown. When I met this designer to show him my portfolio and update him on my recent projects, he told me he really admired the originality of my work and my great sense of aesthetics. A little incredulous, I countered with, "Well, your work is pretty good, too." "Really it isn't," he said.

He opened the bottom drawer of his filing cabinet and showed me a collection of other people's brochures he had stashed over the years, all neatly filed and labeled according to type and industry. He told me he kept everything attractive he came across in case he needed something to copy. Here he was, occupying the top design spot in the city and he didn't have an original thought in his head. What he had was a potpourri of all the best design work in the market to pick and choose from at will. As I came to know from working with him, when he started a new project, he would pull someone else's design work from his reference file and reproduce it right down to the font, paper stock, and color scheme.

The moral of this story is that you should not be intimidated by the big names who market in your area. Fight a good fight when you meet the competition. I can't say it enough: The world is your oyster when your work is good. When you feel intimidated, remember there are plenty of pseudo designers and plagiarizing writers in the fishbowl with you who are not eager to identify themselves.

3. Leverage Your Freelance Advantage

Your advantage as a freelancer is multifaceted. Agencies and studios rarely involve their principals in day-to-day design projects, which can mean only their main clients get their attention. One company hired a well-known Madison Avenue advertising agency to handle their $500,000 advertising campaign. The company's managing partner kept calling the agency for a status report on campaign progress. His calls were rarely returned the same day, and when they were, it was by a junior copywriter. His budget was relatively small compared to the agency's other clients, and his work got the attention of only junior staff, who were delegated to handle it so everybody else could concentrate on the really important clients such as Mercedes and Pepsi.

A medium or small company always benefits by hiring freelancers because the client becomes the center of attention.

What's wrong with this picture? The client hired a major agency based on the agency's reputation and the prestige he thought it would bring to his company. He got a lot of mileage at cocktail parties telling everybody he'd hired a big New York ad agency to handle his company's account. But $500,000 is a lot to pay for boasting rights. He forgot the first rule of the fishbowl — if you want to be a big fish, find a small pond. Clients who want to be treated as if their work is important should hire talent that considers them important because they are the lifeblood of their operation — talent such as freelancers. A medium or small company always benefits by hiring freelancers because the client becomes the center of attention. As a freelancer, take advantage of this and sell yourself as hands-on management. The client who hires a freelance designer has immediate access to creative talent. Of course, when there is no one to pass the buck to, personal diligence becomes even more important. You must commit to and become responsible for your client's happiness.

If you are willing to bend over backwards or jump through flaming hoops to corner the business, make sure you communicate this to potential clients. The upside is that a focused attitude means certain success. Remember, however, that professional relationships don't allow for emoting; there just isn't time. In a portfolio viewing, seize the moment and tell it like it is, because time is short and you may not get another chance. Don't hint that you give good service; just say it outright and make your point. You must say there is nothing more important than your client's project and that it will receive your undivided attention — whether or not this is true. Your client doesn't need to know you have ten other projects. All the client needs to know is that you will finish his project on time and under budget to the best of your ability.

4.   Promote Services via Your Portfolio

The best way to attract attention is to put your best foot forward. If your work is excellent and outshines the competition, show it off. A portfolio presentation is your chance to either show off your excellent work or, if your work's not the best, show off your personality. And don't be surprised if the meeting doesn't go as you expect. I was referred to a new firm by an acquaintance who said: "I've had my fill of working with engineers and I just can't face taking on another one. Would you like to introduce yourself to these guys?" I made an appointment to show my work. Portfolio showings are usually one-on-one meetings in a small cubicle. This time, much to my surprise, I was escorted to a large conference room with more than a dozen businesspeople seated around a big table. I stood at the head of the table and made the usual remarks about each piece as the black mount boards were passed from person to person. At the end of my talk, the principal of the group stood up and thanked me, complimented my work, and said, "And I think everyone will agree with me, it's refreshing to meet someone in your field with a brain." They all chuckled (which made me wonder who was there before me).

Best foot forward means just that. Show your strongest assets and use them to land the work. Business boomed at a local animation studio when management hired a pert blonde and a buxom redhead as client liaisons. In an area rife with gas and oil money, the clients stopped by just to visit and always looked for an excuse to drop off a job with these two. Sex appeal sells in advertising, so if you've got it, flaunt it. Just don't go over the line of common sense and good taste.

Every portfolio presentation is the perfect opportunity to show enthusiasm for the client and the client's project. Do some research on your client's industry and his or her nearest competition. Then spend time putting your best ten sample pieces together (your "book"). Mount them on presentation board and practice what you're going say about each piece. If you can't think of what to say about a particular piece, leave it out. Use each description to convey a sense of enthusiasm for the work and for the experience you had with that particular client. This is also an excellent opportunity to sell creative services by showing how your creativity sold the other client's product or service. Be positive and complimentary.

Every portfolio presentation is the perfect opportunity to show enthusiasm for the client and the client's project.

The presentation will be more interesting if you relay stories and details; to that end, share things you learned by doing each project. This gives the prospective client insight into both your creativity and your professionalism. If you don't have strong language skills, let your work do the talking, pointing out details and focal points as you move from piece to piece.

One last piece of advice: No matter how tempted you are to say something bad about a previous client or professional peer, don't. It will reflect badly on you and your working relationships. Your client will be left with a bad feeling and will associate it with you, not with the subject of your ill will. Speaking negatively will also show your prospective client you don't respect the boundaries of professional courtesy and he may find himself on the other side of a similar rift. *When in doubt, bite your lip.*

How do you decide what to show in your portfolio? Here's where a bit of advance research will pay off. Samples of your work communicate the marketable skills you've accumulated over the course of your career. They should show your versatility, but they should also be relevant to the client's needs. Don't show up for a portfolio presentation without knowing if your skill is being presented to a viable market. Said Barbara Bills, a longtime production manager at a big ad agency, "Kids show up in my office without a clue about how to market themselves, or if I'm even in the market for their skills." Make sure there's a need for what you're selling where you're selling it. Sometimes big agencies will ask you to drop off your book and leave it for a few days. This is common practice at the big-city agencies because, as you probably know, most work is on deadline and successful art directors are often pressed for time. Remember, though, sometimes your book never gets opened, and it might be a good idea to revisit agencies you never hear from. Don't jump to the conclusion that they aren't interested in your work or that they don't need your skill set; it's possible there just wasn't an opportunity open long enough for them to see your work. Many freelance creatives don't succeed simply because they give up as a result of assumptions that don't apply.

Be persistent, keep going back; show you have a solid interest in developing a working relationship and your efforts will usually be rewarded. It also pays to have a promotional mailer ready to send a few days after they've seen your book to remind them that you're available for assignments. Some creatives call it a *leave behind*. Don't leave it behind, but use it as a follow-up mailer within the week. Waiting a few days to remind the client of your visit will reinforce your name and increase the likelihood of getting a first assignment.

For the perfect leave behind, try to create a soft-sell promotional piece that offers something to the recipient and quietly, secondarily, includes your contact information. That's why calendars are popular at Christmastime. Most people keep them around for a year, giving the source free advertising in the process. Apply the same sensibility to your marketing piece and you, too, will create an enduring promotional piece. My promo pieces were always posters with full-size cartoons. They ended up on the wall, nicely framed, where everyone entering could see my name. You can't beat that for continuous promotion around town, and the cartoons always lasted longer than the previous year's calendar.

5. Guidelines for Building a Strong Portfolio

Build your portfolio so it sells your work even when you aren't in the room to provide commentary. Here are some guidelines that will help you choose the right pieces and display them to your best advantage.

5.1 Select ten pieces of your best work

Portfolio showings should be short and sweet. Don't overstay your welcome. For this reason, I suggest selecting no more than ten pieces of your best work for your portfolio. Don't spend time convincing people that you're right for the job. Let your work do the talking.

5.2 Show pieces that promote specific skills

If you are an excellent illustrator, show work that highlights your ability. Don't expect a portfolio filled with strictly editorial design to bring in corporate publication work. If you're particularly creative as a concept copywriter, select pieces that show that skill. Show pieces similar to the type of work you're trying to attract.

5.3 Mount pieces so viewers can see each page

Professional portfolios are easy to create. You don't need a fancy zipper case. Cut ten pieces of black mount board to a manageable size and spray-mount each print piece in the center. This allows "boards" to be exchanged without touching or holding the actual sample. Boards are easily refreshed with a plastic eraser.

5.4 Substitute alternates for special presentations

Customize your portfolio to each presentation by substituting applicable pieces you've done for other clients in the same industry. Prove that you have the skill to do your prospective client's job. If you prepare your alternates ahead of time, customizing your portfolio will be as quick as substituting one board for another. It pays to have a few extra boards cut to size and ready for impromptu presentations. These will facilitate quick substitutions of industry-specific pieces or can serve as replacements when board corners become dog-eared and dented.

The more service you offer, the more likely you will become the vendor of choice for creative services.

5.5 Choose pieces that show off your creativity

Use simple and direct commentary to describe how you participated in each job, and add any information about concept work. The more service you offer, the more likely you will become the vendor of choice for creative services.

5.6 Start with an attention-getter

If your first piece of work is sleepy and dull, you won't hold your audience through the presentation. Use an eye-popping piece to start the show. A sure sign of disinterest is when the client assumes control and does a quick flip. You've lost your audience.

5.7 End with your best piece

Clients will remember you by the last piece they see in the interview, so make sure it's dramatic and leaves a striking impression. Like a great piece of music, end with a crescendo.

5.8 Include a few business cards

Take a small envelope and cut the top off. Spray-mount it to the back of the last board in your portfolio. When the presentation is near an end, hand a business card to your prospect. If you have a brochure promoting your services, save that as a follow-up mailer. Keep your audience's attention on the work in your portfolio, not the depth and scope of services in your brochure.

Sometimes portfolio showings don't go well. Potential clients who keep you waiting far beyond the appointed time or take calls during your presentation are tipping you off to their lack of professionalism. Take this as a warning of what's to come if you keep pursuing their business. I guarantee you will receive the same treatment during the course of the relationship, right up to and including invoices past due. Sometimes this is also a sign of somebody who wants to be nice even though they have no intention of using your services. Spend your time with people who are interested in paying for your services, not those who want to entertain and be entertained.

6. Cultivate a Sense of Humor

If you find yourself in a bad situation, you can always rely on your sense of humor — as I had to do once when I came down hard (literally) during a presentation. After I designed a logo and ad campaign for a recent corporate acquisition, I presented it to my captive audience, who were forced to use my in-house talent because they had already spent $25,000 at a local advertising agency with no results. I introduced the logo and supporting ads, elaborating on my ideas as the boards were passed around the table. When the room grew silent, I could tell by the looks on their faces that I had exceeded their expectations.

Most people can sense when you know what you're doing. A minor objection was raised about verbiage, but I quoted existing literature and the objection was moot. (The more work you complete, the more you see clients with an uncontrollable urge to change something, whether the change is valid or not, just to remind you who's paying the bill.) As I started to sit down at the end of the presentation, my chair rolled out from under me. I fell flat on the floor with my feet straight up in the air — Chevy Chase couldn't have done it better. I looked up from under the table, laughing out loud at my own misadventure. Everybody was relieved I wasn't hurt *and* that it didn't turn into an awkward situation. When your work is good enough to make up for this kind of faux pas, you will have no trouble finding assignments.

If, while giving a presentation, you find a room going silent, accept the silence as praise. There is a scientific basis for the silence when people are enthralled. Language skills resident in the left side of the brain are temporarily inaccessible when emotion takes hold; when you've succeeded at emotionally involving your audience and trapping them in the right side of their brains, they are literally speechless.

I'm not advocating adding slapstick to your presentation, but I want to encourage you to keep a firm grip on your humanity. Creatives have a tendency to take themselves too seriously, with the intention of showing everyone how serious they are about their work. Find the fun in your work and no matter what the circumstance, enjoy yourself. Each day will be filled with adventures beyond your control. You can meet them head on by clenching your teeth or by happily dribbling the ball down the court like a professional, ready for whatever gets thrown at you.

Though creative disciplines don't encourage it, be flexible as a human being, both with yourself and those you deal with. Bad things do happen, and if you act like it's the end of the world, you're probably spending too much time obsessing about mistakes and shortcomings and things you can't change. Do the best you can, and knowing that, will lend solace. Take it from a person who's fallen flat on her ass: The sooner you get up laughing at your own foibles, the sooner you'll move on to your next great adventure and golden opportunity. Or heed a piece of advice from Patrick Dennis's play *Auntie Mame*, "Life is a banquet and most poor suckers are starving to death." Dig in to the smorgasbord.

Find the fun in your work and no matter what the circumstance, enjoy yourself.

Chapter 4

CAPTURING REPEAT CUSTOMERS

After you've done the hard part and accumulated a few steady clients, there are some cardinal rules for keeping them. Let's review the first and foremost rule: Make sure your potential client knows there is no competition for your time, whether or not this is true. The chief rule in business is there are no other clients. One creative director I worked with likened the client-freelancer relationship to a romantic one. "Don't ever let them know you might be spending time on someone else's project," he said. "It makes them jealous."

New business is good to have, but keeping repeat customers is easier and takes a bit of the edge off the unknown (like where your next job is coming from!). A relationship with a client is just like your relationship with your best friend. The only difference is that you might let your best friend see you with spinach between your teeth, whereas your client only wants to see you at your best.

Part of this "best foot forward" strategy is not sharing any trials and tribulations you may experience while completing the job. The only time you should bother your client is if something beyond your control changes the job specifications or budget. Remember, the time you spend with clients is time they take away from building their business. You should also remember there are ten other designers out there waiting to step into your place should you lose the client.

Ask questions; this shows you have a desire to learn the ins and outs of whatever the subject may be.

Work to the best of your ability, and deliver what you promised on time for the price quoted. If you do your job well, your clients will appreciate it and show their appreciation by giving you more work. Take care of your clients and your clients will take care of you. Here are some strategies for keeping your clients coming back for more.

1. Provide Client-Centered Service

Take a few minutes to think about your attitude. Nobody wants to work with a person who sees the project as drudgery. Even the person who removes industrial asbestos for a living takes pride in his or her company and the production of its brochure. He or she has a real interest in how it represents his services and how it will be received by clients and competition.

Ask yourself, why do you want to do this project? The wrong answer is that you need the money to get your cat neutered. The right answer is client-centered: The project is an opportunity to show the client how you can help him promote his business. If you want him to trust you with his project, you must show respect for what he does and the image he wants to project.

Though you may know design, you can never know your client's product or service as well as he does. During your initial pitch, exhibit a willingness to listen, and mirror your prospect's excitement. Ask questions; this shows you have a desire to learn the ins and outs of whatever the subject may be.

1.1 Learn how advertising works

As a freelancer, you will have an advantage over the competition if you offer more than just a pretty design or solid copy. There are a lot of different media competing for your target audiences' time and attention, so you only have a few seconds at best to make a sale. Your work should direct audience eyes, pointing them to exactly what you want them to see or hear, and in what order. Great design controls what the target audience sees, how they see it, and how they retain it. In writing, you have three seconds to deliver the most important message about the product. Can you do it?

If you take your work a step further and move the audience emotionally, you've seriously cornered the market in advertising design. Few designers can manipulate type and image to achieve an emotional reaction in their audience. This goes for writers, too.

Those who have this skill have clients with increased sales and forward-looking business forecasts.

1.2 Become a typography expert

If you haven't achieved this level of expertise but want to, the best time to start is now. Study the best in your field by finding out where they came from and how they arrived. If you're a designer, spend some time developing a keen sensitivity to fonts. Learn who designed them and their history, what they mean, and how not to use them. Become familiar with at least two or three classic selections in each family of fonts that satisfy certain requirements. Study the font design of Herb Lubalin or Ben Franklin, whose work shows the ideal is timeless. Learn what makes one font say "staid reliability" while another font screams "absolute party animal."

Fonts have a more important impact on potential customers than you may realize. This impact is subliminal, as the following story shows. In art school I learned about a hundred-year-old funeral parlor that installed new signage. The owner wanted something bolder and black. After business had declined steadily for about a year, staff surveyed families who had been customers for generations but suddenly were taking their business elsewhere. The participants responded that they had a queasy feeling about the place. They couldn't put their finger on the reason for their unease, but they thought about dead children whenever they saw the funeral home's new sign. The sign company had followed the owner's request and used a big, bold typeface, Cooper Black, the same font traditionally used on children's alphabet blocks.

How confident are you about the fonts you recommend to your clients? Freelancers who are knowledgeable can explain their font choices when presenting project comprehensives. They have the ability and knowledge to guide clients away from poor choices with reason. This is a responsibility that falls under your job description.

1.3 Use appropriate language

Being client-centered also applies if you're a writer. Are you capable of writing using the language of your client's industry? You can't use the same language for a brochure selling industrial starters (a piece of heavy equipment used in oil fields) as for a hip-hop CD blurb. Industry-specific writing is required. Are you capable of communicating effectively in proper jargon? Build your freelance business on a solid set of skills and your business will grow.

2. Decide Where to Position Yourself

The market is made up of all kinds of suppliers, and you should decide where you fit. Depending on your sales ability and the nature of your client roster, you may decide to position yourself as an alternative to the higher-priced design studios and ad agencies. Low overhead and doing most of the work yourself may allow you to charge less. Another aspect of providing low-cost service, as already mentioned, is choosing to do the best job possible for the least amount of money instead of trying to sell your client the most you can. There's never only one way to produce a job, but I guarantee you creatives at some ad agencies and studios sit down and try to figure out how to add extra colors, higher-priced stock, gold foil stamping, embossing, and additional photography in order to increase their commission on each job. This isn't all bad, for truly beautiful and stunning print pieces are produced as a result of the agency's ability to sell. Whether the client sells more widgets is a point well worth debate.

2.1 Pass on cost savings

If you, on the other hand, have an idea that will save your client thousands of dollars without sacrificing quality, suggest it. One firm wanted to put an ad in the PGA golf annual but didn't want to spend a lot of money. I suggested using a photograph I found in a library book instead of setting up a photo shoot. We wrote a letter to the publisher, got permission to use an image of Bobby Jones swinging his golf club, and scanned that photograph. The copywriter discovered through research that the year Bobby Jones won his title was the same year the firm's branch office opened, so it was a stroke of luck that the two coincided. The company ran the perfect ad with a working concept and paid very little for production. A freelancer's creativity when coming up with a concept as well as allocating the budget keeps clients coming back for more. And nothing makes an accountant smile more than a stack of cash he can count again.

2.2 Take the ethical high road

There are times when you may find yourself in an ethical gray area, faced with a couple of choices. There's a man about town who drives a cute sports car because he seized an opportunity when it presented itself — though most people would never cross this ethical line with an employer. His senior position at a major design studio put him in charge of some high-dollar projects. One client was shocked at a high quote and turned a shade of pale gray. The designer sensed that the price did not agree with him and quietly offered to do the job for half of the studio quote on a freelance basis. About a month later when he received payment, he walked into a dealership showroom and paid cash for his new sports car. The downside is he won an award for his design and had a hard time explaining that to his employer.

Remember, if you decide to take the high road (meaning high priced, not high morals) and opt to sell your clients the very best of everything, you will be giving up a marketable advantage as a freelancer. Lower overhead allows you to make a good living without charging top dollar, so plan on leaving some clients behind for those other ten designers ready to step in and do the bread-and-butter work.

Know when to walk away from an unprofitable project or client.

2.3 Focus on your best clients

A veteran in real estate sales taught me an important lesson about productivity. It takes the same amount of time to sell a $40,000 house as it does a $5-million estate — the only difference is the commission. The same applies to freelancing. Courting clients takes time. You will encounter people who want something and need something but don't want to pay a lot or just plain want it for free. Your best clients are the ones who pay what you ask and pay quickly. If somebody who pays slowly wants a rush job and a client who pays in a timely manner also needs your time, give your attention to your best client first. By doing this you will make a good living. Know when to walk away from an unprofitable project or client. But also cultivate a sensitivity to the line your client won't cross or you'll lose him.

2.4 Know who you're working for

Many small companies hire freelancers because they want to get the most for their money, and if you can save them the cost of a blind emboss that does nothing to enhance the value of their brochure, you should. Sometimes using good sense on your client's behalf is ethically correct whether they know the benefit or not. If you buy a lot of beans and get them from a vendor who consistently overcharges, that vendor shouldn't be surprised when he loses the business to someone who charges cost plus a standard markup.

It's up to you to know how to produce the job you just designed.

Gouging because you can get away with it eventually shows up when competitive bids are called for.

When I was working in-house at a major corporation, the CEO had me play the bad guy by keeping his 26 marketing managers from spending too much money on sales literature. He told me every salesperson's excuse for not moving more product was a lack of proper sales literature. "If only I had more color, slicker paper, an extra hundred thousand copies, my name on the bottom, my picture on the left," ad infinitum. Part of my job was to prevent unnecessary expenses and encourage only those expenditures that moved product. Rarely a week went by when someone didn't march into his office and complain about me, "She is so hard to work with." I kept getting raises, the boss kept operating costs down, and the marketing managers were pushed to frustration when it came to producing high-end pocket folders and fancy direct mail pieces.

As an employee, I took instructions from the owner of the company regarding his goals, limitations, and expectations. In fact, my future with *his* company depended on my performance and how I executed his wishes. Different rules apply to a freelancer. Decide whether you want to position yourself as a designer who watches costs and gives good value or one who sells as much material and labor as possible to a client who probably wouldn't know the difference as long as he was pleased with the result. The point is that both positions are tenable and defensible.

As a freelancer, your new-found freedom means you get to define your responsibility. How you guide your clients' spending is up to you, so decide where to position yourself: either as your client's advocate or the advocate of your own profit. Either position is fair, but set your priorities before you find yourself in a situation that requires a decision. Being clear on this will make doing the right thing easier no matter what the circumstances.

3. Learn All You Can about Printing

Another way to look out for your clients' best interests is by being knowledgeable enough to select the right vendor. If you handle clients' printing, keep an eye out for printers who bargain but still do quality work. It's up to you to know how to produce the job you just designed, and that includes knowing which print shops in town have the right equipment to do the job economically and in a technically correct fashion. You don't want to put a four-color job on a single-color press and pay for all the extra make-ready time required any more than you want to put a run of 5,000 on a web-fed press.

If you don't know what I'm talking about, you're not alone. Recent surveys reveal some embarrassing statistics about designers' lack of production knowledge. More people are coming to printers with incomplete files, poorly designed jobs, and jobs that can't be produced. An increasing number of print buyers bring MS Word or Publisher files to their printers instead of Quark or InDesign files. The job may look pretty, but has none of the behind-the-scenes information required for digital printing. According to data from TrendWatch Graphic Arts, the need to train print buyers grew from 7 percent in 2002 to 37 percent in 2003.*

Some printers, bless their little hearts, are now talking in double-speak. They used to complain when jobs came in sloppily prepared and they had to clean up the files prior to printing. Now they talk about helping their customers. The catch is, they are charging for this service and are happy to help in order to make up for the work lost to Print on Demand (POD). Print customers need assistance with color specification, image resolution, and so on, and it is the printer who must dedicate time and money to managing these elements of your job if you come unprepared. The statistics determined by the TrendWatch survey tell an additional story: Work printers are losing to PDF downloads online is being replaced by money generated when the printer turns into a tutor, trying to teach his customers how to prepare a digital file. That's not his area of expertise and I wonder how well he's filling the gap. This trend has added difficulty to the prepress workflow and made even the best system less efficient.

If you understand the relationship between your digital file, the software you're using to prepare it, and how the software relates to the equipment used to produce the printed piece, you can properly prepare your digital files so everybody saves time and money in the end, including your local printer. As a production manager in Los Angeles said: "There is no substitute for experience, as there are so many nuances in production that can only be learned in the trenches. No amount of schooling can cover it."

It's important to learn to use your software to output jobs correctly and in accordance with industry production standards. If you

---

*Report Printing Market Survey 18, Fall 2003, www.TrendWatchGraphicArts.com, quoted from July 21, 2004, e-newsletter distributed by www.PaperSpecs.com.

match the right print equipment to the job and save your client money, well, there just isn't a better freelancer. Learning about paper and how it is made helps, too. Know the difference between a cast coat and a matte finish before you specify a job. It doesn't hurt to know how a coated sheet compares to a text sheet in cost, too, before you make a recommendation. When you learn about a new number two sheet that runs, looks, and feels like a number one sheet, bring it to your clients' attention. As I've already said (and it bears repeating), finding ways to cut costs without giving up quality is part of a freelancer's job.

If your knowledge of digital prepress and printing specifications could be better, I suggest you do one of the following:

- Learn more about the topic by reading (see the CD included with this book for online resources).

- Spend a few hours with a friendly production manager at the nearest print shop.

- Find an online course to help fill in your educational gaps.

- Take a few courses in digital prepress at your local community college.

- Treat yourself to an intensive course from a software company such as Adobe, which holds educational seminars for professionals internationally, or www.lynda.com, an industry favorite available online and at low cost.

If none of these options appeal to you, you might want to leave the production jobs to more qualified freelancers.

Printers have had a long list of trade practices and these are standards accepted industry wide. Usually found on the back of bids, specification sheets and other forms used by a printing company, they list definitions of things like what's included in the price and who owns what. A relatively new term used by digital printers dealing primarily with a public unfamiliar with professional printing standards is "respectable color." When soliciting bids, this term indicates your job will be gang printed. That means the printer will hold your job until he or she has enough work to warrant cranking up the presses at the ridiculously low price quoted. Usually, a "respectable color" job will not have a rapid turnaround as scheduling of jobs has been shifted from the customer's needs to the printers convenience--just as color matching flew out the window. If you have PMS (Pantone Matching System) colors that require matching, the term "respectable color" will let the printer off the hook and you will have no recourse for complaint. This is purely a marketing term used to brush off clients who want a good job but don't want to pay for all the necessary steps required to color match.

Professional designers use comprehensives to show their clients what a particular design will look like prior to investing in printing. They also provide that "comp" to the printer with the files so he or she has a good idea of what the final job should look like; and PMS colors are used to maintain consistency over the many phases of a job. All of these safety nets will be lost if you rely on a printer who uses the term "respectable color" to excuse his or her work.

No matter what you do to fill in what you don't know but should, you will benefit and so will your client. In the final analysis, the more you know, the better off you will be. There's no quicker way to lose a client than to make a mistake on printing specifications and be unable to replace the work at your own expense. If you do make a mistake, be honest about it. During one economic slowdown, I was so distracted that I specified the wrong color for one firm's business cards by one number. It was a minor mistake, but the client called me on it and expected me to correct it. There will be times when circumstances beyond your control will prevent you from righting an obvious wrong. When you want to do the right thing but can't, admit it, say you're sorry, and move on.

Remember to be honest and forthright, within the bounds of good business, and clients will most likely reciprocate.

4. Select Your Partners with Care

Who you partner with on jobs is an important factor in keeping clients — but it is seldom talked about. As in all things involving human beings, you must protect yourself from piranhas — people who cross an ethical line driven by their insatiable urge to have what you've got. They view any job as a job to kill for and don't think twice about stabbing you in the back. Once they gain control of your client, they will go to any length to discredit you and your work. There are piranhas in every profession and quite a few the freelancer has to subcontract with. (For more on these, see Chapter 11.) But there are certain things you can do to protect yourself. The first is a good line of communication. Remember to be honest and forthright, within the bounds of good business, and clients will most likely reciprocate. If you suspect controlling or underhanded behavior, confront the culprit, warn them about your suspicions and their potential loss of work in the future, then complete the job as quickly as possible. Never let the client know there's a problem

Whether your artwork is prepared on a board or saved in a digital file, never let it out of your control.

unless the situation is unsalvageable. Learn from your experience and sever that questionable alliance quietly and without animosity.

Of course, sometimes your choice of partner is beyond your control. Even then, you need to be on the lookout for unethical behavior. One of my longtime clients enjoyed racquetball. He asked me to design a brochure with copy written by his racquetball buddy, a copywriter. I had a long-standing working relationship with this client and didn't give it a second thought when the copywriter's assistant asked me to send her the art boards for proofreading. Pay attention now, because piranhas are very smooth and their teeth are so sharp, you won't know you've been bitten until you've bled to death. "I will be sending you copies of the boards no later than tomorrow," I told the copywriter's assistant. She sounded slightly perturbed on hearing this and pointed out that they wanted the boards, not copies. I stood fast and told her I would send her copies, which would have everything on them exactly as shown on the paste-up. She was now clearly frustrated and said, "This is *our* client and we need the boards to handle the printing."

At this point I had to either stand my ground or back off and resign myself to giving up a substantial printing commission. I informed her that I had done this client's work for many years and had no intention of handing over production responsibility for a job I had designed. As soon as I hung up, I called my client. Ordinarily you shouldn't involve clients, but you do need to clarify their wishes. In this case, I made sure my client only wanted the copywriter to write copy — not produce the brochure.

Whatever happens, you must respect your client's wishes. Politics impact many business deals, and your client may be paying back a favor or two behind the scenes. My client understood my concern completely and reassured me that I was handling his brochure as usual. The copywriter remained just that: a minor contributor. The lesson is, whoever controls the files controls the job. Whether your artwork is prepared on a board or saved in a digital file, never let it out of your control. If I had not had a good relationship with my client, I would not have been comfortable calling him for clarification, and I might have inadvertently stepped on his toes as well as losing the printing commission. That said, always investigate innuendo, for assumptions can lead to incorrect judgments and wrong calls.

5. Keep in Touch with Clients

To maintain your relationship and keep what I call the "awkward-ness of unfamiliarity" at bay, call your client once in a while when there's no work just to touch base. A quick call to let them know you're available for assignments serves you both as long as it's brief. Don't be aggressive, as this won't serve you well in your field. Designers and writers are sophisticated, elegant people as a group, and behaving like a cretin will do you more damage than good. An email will work just as well as a phone call and is sometimes less disruptive, as any overworked executive will tell you. The idea is to keep your work or your presence in a comfortable place of accessibility without being a pest. Remind your client that you are there to serve. If that bothers you, remember those ten freelancers waiting to take your place. You'll snap right out of it.

An alternative and perhaps more gentle reminder is a promotional mailing. I did a brisk business in cartoons and made a regular practice of sending out posters in mailing tubes. Some of my clients collected them and displayed them proudly in their offices. Mailing tubes attract attention when they arrive and will more likely get opened than another number ten envelope in a stack of junk mail. One day I ran to the front door to keep the mail carrier from shoving ten pounds of mail through the narrow mail slot. "Are you the famous artist who painted *Melon at the Plaza*?" he asked. This was a pen-and-ink cartoon I had done as a mass mailing. "I've got your painting [*sic*] over my sofa in the living room. We just love it." I asked him how he had received it. He told me bulk mail that's undeliverable is thrown out, but the postal employees loved my cartoons so much they kept them. Promotion of any kind is never a waste of time when you freelance, so promote yourself profusely. (See section **9.** later in this chapter for more marketing ideas.)

6. Recognize and Avoid Problem Accounts

Not all clients will be worth placating, but sometimes you won't know this until you are involved in a job. Here are some tips on recognizing, handling, and avoiding "problem" clients. You may encounter clients who take advantage and start demanding more than you're willing to give. Some of the worst offenders are previous employers who act as if they're doing you a favor by giving you

It is much better to walk away from a job than lose control of the finished product.

freelance work. Frequently they expect you to do it for the same hourly rate you received as an employee. They knew you when you worked for $25 an hour and just can't see the logic in the rate you charge now. Sometimes giving more than you get is required, especially when working with the nonprofit sector. But even this has its limits, as the following story illustrates.

When I was well established and had several regular clients, I did a lot of work for a large parochial school. With each assignment came the message that they only used designers who knew they had to give a little to get a little. I swallowed this hook, line, and sinker because I really enjoyed working with the director of admissions. But when a different staff member asked me to work up a layout and then refused to pay because she had changed her mind, I drew the line. When you find yourself in such a situation, do whatever you can to complete the current project to the best of your ability. The next time the abusive client calls with a job, politely decline due to an overloaded schedule.

You never know who will have the next $50,000 design project, so don't make an enemy. But don't waste any time worrying about jobs you don't get from clients who don't want to pay. Unrealistic expectations are a continuing, industry-wide problem. Companies expect innovative work but don't allow for it in the annual budget. Most marketing people have limited knowledge of production costs. They don't know, for instance, that adding a fifth color will add 25 percent to the budget. Unrealistic expectations can lead to the client being disappointed and blaming the designer, when really the problem was in planning.

6.1 Clients you can live without

You don't need clients who expect you to work for minimum wage, delay payment for months (especially on rush jobs), or act like they're doing you a big favor by giving you work. Clients who try to get you to give more than you're being paid for by dangling the carrot of a future job in your face often can't afford you. They want your work but don't want to pay for it. They may try to weasel out of paying for one reason or another as the job winds down. When you get your business established, you can politely walk away from clients who dangle those mythical carrots in your face or who never want to spend enough to do the job right.

One woman was so enamored of my color comps, she became physically aggressive and tried to rip them out of my arms on the day of the photo shoot, grabbing for the boards as I walked out the door. She wouldn't spend the money to do the job right and had, without telling me, hired a wedding photographer to shoot product shots that required highly technical lighting. I told her I would not risk my professional reputation and refused to hand over the comps when she wanted to do her own art direction. Incorporating shoddy photography in a brochure is a quick way to reduce overall quality. You must take responsibility for the end result of your work; whatever you produce will affect your reputation for as long as the piece circulates. It is much better to walk away from a job than lose control of the finished product.

6.2 It's all about standards

The only thing that really separates you from the competition is your standards. It's great to be easy to work with, but how long can you survive with shoddy work following you from place to place? One almost-famous copywriter in New York says the real freedom of freelancing is your ability to walk away from difficult clients without suffering the ire of the boss. Walking away from a client who thinks his art direction and type selection are superior to yours is no sacrifice in the long haul.

Are you willing to maintain standards in the face of criticism or difficulty? Here are some questions to ask yourself as you decide what your professional standards will be:

- In the face of a design or contract dispute, is this a client you can afford to lose? Is the client more important than your work?

- Are you willing to roll over and forsake your integrity as a designer in exchange for money?

- Can you identify bad clients and muster the courage to tell them to take their business elsewhere?

Your answers to these questions will determine the nature of the service you render and how happy you will be as a freelance creative. In the end, your standards are what make real clients who respect what you do flock to your door. They know a happy creative does excellent work and they aspire to it. Integrity that won't bend says a lot about your self-esteem and character, not to mention your productivity.

All businesses have clients they look forward to hearing from as well as those they can't stand. For the ones you like, do everything you can to cement the relationship. Redemption for the ones you can't stand is the money they pay for services rendered. Add an agony fee for truly difficult clients if it makes you feel better. You're the boss.

7. Seek Honest Feedback

Look for truthful criticism so you know the true nature of your standing among your peers. Awards and plaques are not a good measure because the sometimes heady entry fees may be cost-prohibitive. Find someone who knows the business and will be honest with you. This practice served me well over the years. Just to keep in practice, I would periodically make an appointment to show my portfolio to one creative director who I knew spoke his mind. At one particular showing, I apologized for the poor choice of words in a headline, explaining it was changed at the last minute by the client. "So, in other words, you rolled over instead of doing the right thing," he said.

I cringed and shuffled my feet, looking for escape from the ugly truth. I had mixed feelings about that "truth," because I had been accused of being hard to work with in the past. Defending myself, I said, "But it was the client's wish and I had to do what he wanted or risk losing him." The creative director said pointedly, "You didn't want to risk losing your client, so instead you risked losing your reputation. Uh-huh."

This creative director taught me that part of my role as creative talent, freelance or otherwise, was to educate. "Part of your job is to persuade and if you can't persuade, then you need to walk away and let somebody else do the job who *can* persuade them to do it right," he said. That's the ideal, and you can practice it if you have a long list of paying clients. The reality of freelancing is you will be more successful if you please your client on all fronts. The person who signs the check usually determines who gets the job. That person is not going to hire someone who perpetually argues on the side of excellent design when all the client wants is exactly what he wants.

Learn to read your clients and know how to tell the difference between those who want you to do an excellent job (and that's why they hired you) and those who want you to do what you're told. The latter have no rhyme or reason for their requirements, and working for them is a nightmare. They are the micro-managers of the world, who subscribe to the axiom "If you want it done right, do it yourself." This works as well in design as it does when prescribing your own corrective lenses — NOT! Agree to give in to a client's wishes whenever possible, but be prepared to walk away from that client when you are unable to convince him that good design is more important than following orders.

8.   Be Flexible but Not a Doormat

It's true some creatives are denigrated to become merely a pair of hands on a keyboard, taking dictation for every typographic function, the structure of every sentence, and each design program trick. In this case, they contribute only a willing attitude. Is that what you think your job is as a creative?

As a creative, you are obligated to strive for originality and push the envelope.

The truth of today's marketplace is that you will have to make some hard choices if you want to eat regularly, like working for dictatorial clients if you can grit your teeth and bear it. Some clients only expect you to do what you're told, and their brochures show the limitations of their design education. (Remember, that limitation will follow you wherever you go.)

Don't allow yourself to become a design flunky, no matter how much you need the work. Clients may hire you because they don't know how to use layout software to create a design and may not be interested in your input. They may expect you to execute their ideas and not to contribute. They may greet input as interference and not have a clue why using their favorite cursive typeface in the new company logo isn't a good idea. These are clients you (and your reputation) can do without. You can identify them by the following characteristics:

- They don't understand the concept of hiring a professional to do the job right.

- They believe anyone they hire should be told what to do.

- They think hiring a professional will enable them to do what *they* want to do *professionally*.

Because there are clients like this, there is so much bad advertising. One prime example: A well-known chewing gum manufacturer is notoriously rigid about how his product is portrayed and *exactly* how he wants it sold. You've probably seen the TV commercials with the outdated jingles and silly "walks in the park." Until this business owner allows the experts to bring his product into modern times, he'll be stuck with a small portion of his potential market and absolutely dated, forgettable advertising. The bottom line is that it's his product and if he wants to handle it that way, it's

As a freelancer, you have the license to be innovative when attracting the attention of your clients.

nobody's business. Literally. It's nobody's business (creatives won't invest emotionally) because it's more trouble than it's worth. Creative shops have stopped pitching and only rollovers line up when the account is up for grabs. This happens frequently, since the business owner can't figure out why he grows tired of his own advertising so quickly.

The average client, unlike most creatives, doesn't suffer under the yoke of striving to push design standards a rung higher. As for know-it-all clients, one marketing manager explained such uninformed authority as the result of being inundated with advertising and print. "The average person sees so much of it, they subscribe to the misconception that they can produce it," remarked Theron Morrow, a product manager for a national company. As a creative, you are obligated to strive for originality and push the envelope. Without this drive, you are merely producing, not creating.

One client became angry when I told him he wouldn't be able to update his new brochure himself. He implied that I had done this on purpose to keep him from making his own changes (therefore forcing him to hire a designer!). I told him his complaints should be directed toward the software developers and gave him directions to the nearest FedEx / Kinko's photocopy shop, the perfect solution for the do-it-yourselfer.

In the end, there is no profit or enjoyment in working for a combination control freak/cheapskate, no matter how well the money spends. When a do-it-yourselfer reveals himself, take advantage of your freedom and walk the walk. Such clients do not deserve the advantages creativity brings to their projects and should suffer the results of their own work.

9. Get Creative with Your Marketing

After you hone your skills and decide which ones to base your business on, the next step is marketing yourself. I promise you will fail if you have great skills and don't tell anyone. However, if you feel shy about setting out, start online. If you follow the tried-and-true tips in this book (see Chapter 5), this is the only marketing you will need to do if your work is good.

There's other fun to be had, though. You can create unique marketing programs to get your name on the tips of clients' tongues. As a freelancer, you have the license to be innovative when attracting the attention of your clients, especially if they enjoy creative energy. Let the engineers of the world restrict their work to dry, conservative brochures. As an artist, your creativity is limited only by your courage.

Most of my clients receive a big plate of homemade Christmas cookies from me every year, and every one of them look forward to it as the years pass. The gift is simple but effective. You might think this idea is silly (the competition was always more sophisticated), but cookie dough is just another form of art material. If you use your creative skills, they'll be admired no matter what the medium. One meringue cookie looked exactly like a mushroom, and when I handed over the plate one year, a client said, "I see you included some fresh mushrooms for low-carb eaters." I knew none of the commercially prepared cheese trays and fruit baskets got nearly as much attention as my "visual feast for the eyes," and you can be sure the next design project had my name on it. Of course, you can always rely on the more traditional direct mail, but why not put your creativity to work just as hard for yourself as you do for your clients?

On a brief break, I spent the weekend at the Plaza Hotel in New York City with friends and visited some museums. When I got back, I found it hard to explain to friends the bizarre way the hotel had served cantaloupe at breakfast. I drew a cartoon to show how silly the unripe melon looked perched on a silver pedestal filled with ice, then placed on a slick porcelain plate. To top it off, the serving staff had given me a spoon to eat the melon; this was a comic farce waiting to happen. My impromptu sketch turned into a wonderful cartoon (the aforementioned *Melon at the Plaza*) and became a client favorite when I printed up posters and mailed them out for promotion. Even my Uncle Sam could clearly see the correlation between the museum trip and the research required to do the cartoon to justify that tax deduction.

10. Treat Your Clients Royally

Share the good times. Be happy to see your clients no matter where you run into them. I was in Toronto one week for business and coordinated my return with the arrival of one of my clients, with the help of his secretary. This Texas multimillionaire, a commercial real estate broker, was attending a big convention by himself. His secretary confided in me that he had never been to Toronto and was a little timid — he hated strange places. I was familiar with the client's bawdy sense of humor, having worked with him for more than six years, and rose to the occasion. I hired a stretch limousine for the day, made my way to the airport early, and expected to board my plane shortly. I stopped at my client's terminal first, waited discreetly for him to deplane, then quietly walked up behind him. I slid my arm into his and said, "Hey, baby, you want a ride?" At first, well, you know what he thought. But as soon as he recognized me, he put on a big grin, evidently happy to see a familiar face in a strange place.

"I've arranged a little ride for you, my dear," I said as I winked. I took him by the arm and led him out to the unexpected limo. "You mean this is mine for the whole day?" He was positively gleeful. I introduced him to the driver and told him to take care of him. That's how you get your client to associate you with happy times and not just work, as any good salesperson will tell you. Have fun, enjoy yourself, and your client will, too.

Another long-term client gave me particular satisfaction whenever I made his notorious stone face crack a smile. His partner frequently got a good laugh during photo shoots as I struggled to make him relax. He was a retired naval aviator who had recently quit smoking, a stressful endeavor at best and certainly no incentive to relax. Knowing he enjoyed the finer things, I sent him a particularly distinctive gift every year on his birthday.

At precisely two in the afternoon, a butler dressed in a tuxedo with white gloves and tails (a professional actor) would appear with a silver tray, some Baccarat crystal, and a bottle of Phillipe de Rothchild champagne chilled to perfection. The first time, of course, I sent two glasses and joined him to toast the occasion, then quickly took my leave so he could enjoy the elegance of the moment. This sent the staff scurrying to watch the show. As the years passed this annual event became something not only he, but also his staff looked forward to, and it was always met with a round of applause.

An important note: If you want to be successful at this sort of unusual adventure without disturbing your client's business day, it is imperative that you coordinate with another trusted principal or a loyal, yet discreet, assistant. People who love their bosses are usually eager to assist, and as long as you have the courage, you should execute any idea that suits your personal style and cements client relationships. Remember that creative promotion is never limited to two dimensions and the world is, indeed, a stage.

Chapter 5

IDENTIFYING AND TARGETING YOUR MARKET

1. Marketing Using the 4Ps: Product, Price, Place, and Promotion

Sometimes marketing people seem more interested in doing my job than their own. They yearn for the fun stuff; what they don't realize is it's only fun when an expert is doing it. Like watching a professional ice skater, it looks easy until you don the skates and land flat and hard on the ice. Marketing lands flat and hard in art direction, so I'll share a few things I've learned about the 4Ps to keep marketing focused on their marketing jobs. Use these examples to lead them by the nose back to what they should be doing. You can also apply what you learn about the 4Ps to marketing your skills as a professional designer.

Marketing students are educated in the four Ps: product, price, place, and promotion. I don't have to tell you they sometimes get confused, especially about the last one, thinking they have all the skills necessary to concept and create promotional stuff because they took a couple of graphics courses in school. Knowing the Ps will help you keep your marketing co-workers focused on working within their skill set instead of trying to mess around with yours.

1.1 Product

What exactly is your product? A seasoned professional and highly efficient production manager for more than a few big ad agencies in her time told me, "I get lots of calls from freelancers who want to show portfolios and I'm always glad to give them a few tips when I have time. But sometimes, I am absolutely baffled when they show up with no idea what they're selling. They aren't sure what their specialty is; they like doing one thing but have no samples. They want logo work, but they design silly little detailed logos that no one would be able to reproduce. Didn't anybody tell them that a corporate identity has to work in print as well as on the web?"

Before you go out marketing your services, make sure you know what you want to sell.

This is an easy task. Take a few days to think about what you enjoy doing most, and then consider what you do best. If the two coincide, deciding what services to sell will become clear. Art directors and production managers in ad agencies want to know which of their needs you can satisfy. Can they count on you for illustration, concept work, corporate identity, or publication design? Are you fast and efficient in production? Learn to think of your skill as a product with features and benefits for the person buying your service. Neither here nor there, your service is the product traded for currency. Your customers want your work, you want their money; so a trade is made. This is called THE OFFERING.

One of the reasons it's so hard to get your foot in the door is all the bad work out there. Agencies are flooded with unqualified and poorly educated portfolio bearers asking for time to show their work. There is always a gauntlet to pass through; a secretary who knows little about what you do but who still must determine if you're worth the time, or a desperate production artist who is the bottom of the rung and sees every freelancer as competition. These folks are stopgaps in a big agency's desperate effort to invest the minimum amount of time wading through a sea of hopefuls. If you are gifted and your work is well worth their time, you must suffer through the mess that's been created by the mass of wannabes and hope your talents are clearly evident. It pays to be nice to everyone, even those whose job it is to keep you out. Sometimes, you may not get seen and that is the real injustice of the system. Play the game, be persistent and always do periodic follow-up; including dropping off recent samples with your business card and a note attached. Something as simple as "Just off the press — wanted to update you on my recent work. Give me a call if you need some help." This won't work if your portfolio is filled with sloppy, unprofessional, or unresolved work.

Take the time to define the characteristics of your service; make sure you meet the needs of your clients while you're at it. Don't forget service, support, and warranty. That old saying, "The customer is always right," is no longer true. Like common sense, reasonable expectations are no longer common. A recent case in point is the Chung family's dry cleaning business, and how they misplaced a pair of pants owned by a judge who sued them for $54 million based on their "Satisfaction Guaranteed" sign. The test of reasonableness is frequently applied to injury cases; is it reasonable to find a chicken bone in chicken salad? Yes. Case dismissed. An Associated Press news story on the verdict quoted Judge Judith Bartnoff when she ruled that the Korean immigrant owners of Custom Cleaners did not violate the city's Consumer Protection Act by failing to live up to Roy L. Pearson's expectations of the "Satisfaction Guaranteed" sign that was placed in the store window. Judge Pearson must now pay the Chungs everything they spent protecting themselves against his frivolous lawsuit, and he gets the pants, which they found and tried to return earlier.

Most Internet service providers will allot you space for a website as part of your access agreement.

1.2 Price

Is the price right or is it out of sight? In the best of worlds, product launches are thoughtful, labor intensive risk-taking ventures with marketing strategies firmly in place. Before investing in a new venture, the four key marketing factors are carefully defined. Get any one of these wrong, and results will be less than stellar. Whether it's widgets, consumer goods, or professional services, knowing the 4Ps will allow you to achieve maximum results with minimum effort.

Ethics should be a part of pricing, but that is not always the case. Here's an example; genital herpes is a painful, recurrent, and debilitating disease that still has no cure. When a repressive agent for the disease was discovered, a marketing team used focus groups to decide price. Questionnaires asked, "How much would you pay for relief from this condition?" Respondents answered "$100 a day," and, "Everything I have." The questionnaire continued with price

Remember, the image you create for yourself is just as important as the work you do for a client.

ranges, feeling out the market for how much is too much and what the market would bear.

Let's take it one step further and ask, if you were dying, how much money would you pay to stay alive? The exchange of money for curing human ills is a sordid business. It would be interesting to know how they determined the price of the new cervical cancer vaccination that must be renewed each year. How many days this year would you like to be protected from cancer? Would a dollar a day be too much? Sheer unjustifiable extortion, an assumption that poor people don't have lives worth saving, or something else?

A popular topic of conversation on message boards and forums is price — how much should I charge for what I do? Setting the right price is very important when marketing professional design services. Set it too low, and you may lose potential clients who suspect shoddy work for bargain prices. Book writers without real world experience have some radical ideas about freelance fees including suggesting you use the average income of a full time designer in a corporation as a basis — an annual income that has no bearing on your expenses, range of projects, or reasonable price expectations in your practice area. Base your charges on the range of services you offer and juggle that against your level of expertise and education; with a pinch or two for taxes, overhead, and a bit for that yacht. Also consider that a well-educated, seasoned designer can produce more quality work in an hour than a novice who is still learning. A client shouldn't have to pay for time spent figuring out how to do the job, or trying a dozen or more typefaces at random because of uncertainty.

If you still aren't sure about how much to charge, try an anonymous poll with competitors in the area by putting out a small job for bid. What should you say? You've got a small job you're subcontracting out. Remember to consider skills, speed, and know-how when comparing yourself to the competition. Be careful to include your cost of living — a freelancer in New York City or San Francisco should charge a great deal more than a designer in Beaumont, Texas, because overhead is higher. In general, when setting pricing parameters, don't rely on prices quoted in books or you'll price yourself right out of work. A unique style and experience require a price that reflects the value-added services you provide. Don't cast pearls before swine by selling yourself on the cheap, and never work for free. Visit the www.no-spec.com site every time you feel weak in the knees and find yourself thinking of working for free.

Anyone charging $25 an hour to create original art makes me wonder where they rank themselves among professional services and trades. Even in rural areas, plumbers charge $75 an hour plus a service fee. "Lady, it's $50 just to see my face, then it's additional for the work." Attorneys charge upwards of $450 an hour. Is knowing how to unclog a sink or understanding the law much different from all the knowledge required to take a project from concept to print or develop a corporate identity? I think basing the value of design work on sheer sweat and knowledge alone must demand a high premium especially since we're producing original art. Custom prices for custom work; and don't forget to add that 15 percent sales commission for outside services like printing.

1.3 Place

Let's discuss place. A clear understanding of the strategy behind place (or positioning) is all you need to make it work for you; even if it's just to see through the mist some marketers use to fog up discerning shoppers.

I worked with an Englishman and I looked forward every day to hearing his ever-so-eloquent pronunciation drip like sweetness from a perfectly ripe honeydew melon. Having a drab Midwestern accent makes me appreciate anyone with a bit of regional character. He argued with me about what the 4Ps meant; I didn't have the heart to tell him that positioning had nothing to do with ad placement on a page. Here are a few examples of positioning. See how you can use positioning to your advantage either for yourself or your clients.

I am a totally weird shopper. There's nothing wrong with spending top dollar on things that matter; computers, iPods, software, fine Italian shoes even. But when it comes to things like vacuum cleaner bags, well, I used to look to the "low price leader" for the lowest price. I'm not going to give anyone free advertising here, especially if their positioning is a big fat lie. This particular store is so protective of their positioning, they evicted a product comparison shopper from their stores, saying their pricing was proprietary. When temperatures are looming around the mid-fifties (Fahrenheit), low-end air conditioners are $78; and after watching the low price

You can get great visibility immediately and for free by either mounting your work on a website or putting together a PDF portfolio.

leader's TV ads, you might expect that price to go down. But nooo (Steve Martin Style, please) — as the temperature rises, so, too, does the price of an air conditioner. Positioning has nothing to do with reality. Marketing managers decide where they want to compete in the market and control their image accordingly. Positioning tells your target how to think about you, sometimes accomplished by using an effective tagline like low price leader even though it has nothing to do with reality.

It was big news when the low price leader announced generic prescriptions for $4 a month. All the people on fixed incomes were excited and hopeful that finally their prescription costs would be manageable. What they found out was there was a limited list of generics that were available for $4, and those only included 20 pills. I personally haven't had a month with only 20 days, so it's no wonder they didn't include that information in their ads or on the multitude of news reports that extolled the program.

Positioning is about painting a pretty picture of how you want people to think of your product or company; the catchphrase should be simple, easy to remember, and satisfy the audience enough so that they won't look too closely at the wicked web you could be weaving. One of the jobs I held while I worked my way through school was at a data entry job in a major retailer. That lovely Ellie Tahari skirt I wanted was purchased from the manufacturer for $12 but retailed for $75. Now when I see a department store advertising up to 75 percent off end-of-season items, well, that's no big deal. It also taught me that my peers in the design industry who consider the trade mark-up practice on printing and other sub-contracted purchases underhanded and unethical haven't got a clue about the way the rest of the world conducts their business. Just a reminder; the standard mark-up should be the gross times 0.1765, which will give you 15 percent of the gross, not the net. Take your profit because you earned it, and remember that agencies frequently mark stuff up as high as 45 percent.

There are all kinds of good examples of positioning; another can be found on an insurance website that advertises price comparisons with the competition. That insurance company's policies often cost hundreds of dollars more than the caveman/gecko brand, which conveniently is not included in the comparison.

1.4 Promotion

Chindoya street performers used to be a given when promoting the opening of a new pachinko parlor. Pachinko is a popular arcade game in Japan, and if you know the rules, you can make big bucks by cashing in your little steel balls for the right premium. Promotions attract attention, even if it is just the chin and don sounds of a Chindoya band's instruments. Discerning between a marketing promotion and designing promotional materials is frequently an issue for in-house corporate designers. "I am the marketing manager, therefore, I control everything about this product, especially the promotion, and that includes advertising design." Whoa, horsey. Management pays too much attention to marketing managers and too little attention to separating personal preferences from professional choices when formulating product parameters. You know that old Stan Freberg song, "Betsy Ross and the Flag: Everybody Wants to be an Art Director," well, some of the lyrics go, "Everybody wants to be an art director, everybody wants to call the shots." Art directors and designers unite: Only you have been adequately trained to make decisions concerning aesthetics, so don't let your marketing manager get giddy with power when it comes to promotion. You're not doing him or her or your company any favor by rolling over and playing dumb while marketing calls the aesthetic shots. Promotion is not about choosing typefaces, working up concepts, or designing ads. Promotion refers to the program used to stimulate demand for a product.

One very reliable promotion: Calendars are one of the oldest, most trusted methods of promotion, no matter what the business, product, or service. There's a reason for that; staying power. Few people can discard a calendar; ask an older, male mechanic where he used to get his favorite free babe calendar and he'll probably remember Snap-On-Tools® or another brand well enough to think of the brand when he needs new tools. Calendars are common promotions because they stick around for at least a year, but if you're self employed, they might be a bit costly to produce on a large format offset press; at least I thought so when I first started freelancing. For my very first self-promotion, I wanted something nice I could give to my clients that they would keep; something that didn't die when the end of the year came around, and something equally appealing as a reminder after a cold call or portfolio showing. That's when I started a regular series of self-promotional posters; starting with *Melon at the Plaza, NYC* which you can download for free on my website; www.sdkirkland.com. I mailed each one in a tube so it would be hard to ignore. It was reassuring to see it nicely framed and prominently displayed everywhere I went. That was before cyber times; now all you have to do is create a PDF file that can be downloaded at will. Self-promotion is easier and cheaper than ever.

When creating a promotion for your product, concentrate on motivating your target market and put yourself in their place. What type of offer will motivate your target? Airlines have great promotions when they open a new hub, such as one airline's $89 airfare to Las Vegas. A limited time promotion always attracts attention, both from the market and the competition. What kind of leverage will you provide to salespeople that will motivate them to sell your product over the competition? One cell phone company has offered to buy out your current contract if you sign up with them. What kind of deal will you create that will seem like an offer your target can't refuse? Advertising, public relations, and publicity will keep your product or service out front, ahead of the competition; and these are all parts of promotion.

How does advertising differ from promotion? Advertising is supposed to get everybody's attention. Signs, brochures, videos, direct mail, email campaigns, corporate blogs, and community events all fall under the fourth P of promotion. So the next time a marketing manager steps in with specific instructions regarding promotional materials, remind him or her that his or her job is strategy, not application. And I want to be a fly on the wall when you suggest that the marketer's dabbling in graphics at college did not equip him or her with what's required to be a professional designer. And, no, redecorating a bathroom does not qualify as design experience.

1.5 The 4Ps extended to 7 to Include the Service Sector

Marketing has an advantage over design; they have studies, strategic planning, and numbers to back up what they do. Hard facts are handy things when it comes to expenditures and raises — it's what bean counters understand. They can draw conclusions from marketing research not clearly evident in the subliminal pushes and pulls of design. Marketing people don't make statements like, "That's how I feel" when justifying a design decision. "There are "marketing studies" related to design and design elements, if designers choose to use them," says Richard Laurence Baron, a veteran B2B Creative Director in Houston. "While I haven't checked lately, AIGA often reveals various studies that can be of assistance ... or not. The challenge with studies involving designers and design is, of course, that we (the marketing communications community) frequently generate emotion-based rather than numbers-based work: we feel something is correct or beautiful. To rely on studies may stamp us as uncreative. Eye-motion studies and stylistic evaluations (for example) can occasionally reveal what works and what doesn't ... most of the time. Nothing can replace good instincts though — and following your good instincts can lead to remarkable results."

The 4Ps were introduced in the mid 1960s — to update this old but good theory, progressive minds adjusted the Ps to accommodate technological changes in the global marketplace. The 4Ps can be used in your own business and as an adjunct to the old axiom, knowledge is power. In the sections that follow, read about the three new Ps: people, process, and physical evidence.

Edit your introductory letter so that it relates to the industry you're targeting.

1.6 People

The *Booms and Bitner Journal* expanded McCarthy's marketing strategy tool in 1981 to include the service industry and services like design. Part of the success equation in any service industry is PEOPLE. A rude waiter at a posh restaurant can ruin an expensive meal; just as an incorrectly burned DVD is an inconvenience and delay to what might have been an otherwise successfully completed job. For that matter, your knowledge base as a designer also plays a part in the quality of service you deliver. People are part of the marketing methodology — everyone associated with the production and delivery of the service plays an integral part in the success of their business.

Whether you manage the process, create or package the product, deliver the final proofs or simply answer the phone, the weakest link might sink a service business. So, mind your humanity.

1.7 Process

Like printers who cling to antiquated stripping procedures, registering negs on sheets of goldenrod, there are still a few typesetters clinging to the fantasy that people will abandon their computers and straggle back to professional typesetting. These kamikaze dreamers have stifled their own business growth by ignoring technological changes; and that's where process comes in. If you're still sitting at a drawing table with your exacto and a wax machine, creating keylines with your rapidiograph and charging your client for

Time is the one thing everybody gets to spend only once.

the long hours you spend while the rest of the competition produces more perfect jobs on a computer, you are not paying attention to process. In widget manufacturing, they came up with the ISO9002 standards so manufacturers can measure and improve processes, keeping up with new technologies in their particular industry. In our service industry, procedures like client conferences, initial roughs, and print dummies will always be used to control the process. No matter how much technology changes our tools, we will still submit final proofs to clients for approval and signature. It's a proven process that clearly delineates liability.

1.8 Physical Evidence

In case you haven't heard, the DC judge who sued his cleaners for $56 million for losing his pants filed an appeal in spite of being brought before the Bar Association. You can spot a dry cleaner by the traffic — cleaning being dropped off and picked up, equipment you see and hear, and by the business's reputation. There is PHYS-ICAL EVIDENCE that the business has the capacity to provide the service. Your tangible evidence is a portfolio filled with samples of work and maybe a list of references from previous clients. All that computer equipment and high-end design software is also tangible, physical evidence that you can provide a service. Equipment alone is no guarantee, though, as we all know a few people who bought the equipment and studied the software manuals without having a lick of design expertise.

The intangible part of physical evidence is the experience of your existing customers, their level of satisfaction, and your ability to relay that satisfaction to potential clients. Yes, it's true that a good line of slick talk will help you find new clients and build a rigorous business in spite of all other factors. Unfortunately, intangible slick talk coupled with tangible equipment still won't help you deliver that intangible client satisfaction required to be a success in the cre-ative services field. As any person will tell you, a tool is just a tool, even if it is a charming one. Knowing how to use the tool is the single determining factor in achieving satisfaction.

Before the age of the web, starting a freelance business meant printing business cards and handing them out while cold-calling as many clients as possible. It meant talking up friends and neighbors looking for the wayward project and hanging out at the local print shop. The Internet has changed the marketplace completely, lifting restrictions such as locale and the number of miles you could cover in a day. In the past, whatever industry thrived in an area was where freelancers found their business. Now the world is literally the freelancer's oyster. The only thing preventing you from doing business all over the globe is your limited imagination. Granted, some companies prefer local talent, but they, too, like indispensable typesetters before computers, will eventually be dragged into the cyber era kicking and screaming.

Change is hard for everyone, but it's better to be at the front of the pack when change hits rather than lingering behind as your business moves out of reach and over to the competition. If you don't see the web as access to a global market, you will never be part of it. So open your mind to the possibilities.

2. Take Advantage of Today's Opportunities

At the advent of computers in commercial art, forward-thinking typesetting companies were already making plans to revamp their services so they wouldn't be left "holding the bag" as fewer and fewer designers bought galleys of type. Other typesetters, slow to realize the new technology would make them obsolete and slow to offer replacement services such as high-resolution output, figured they had cornered their part of the printing market and had nothing to worry about. That's what Polaroid thought, too, before the introduction of digital cameras.*

Being left "holding the bag" is waking up one day to find that all your captive clients now have computers that can do almost the same thing they used to pay you to do. Typesetters who didn't move with the times are still sitting around asking themselves, "So, what do I do *now* to make a living?" (Most "typesetters," as they were called, are now strictly output agencies. But their situation is still precarious, for printers are taking disks and either outputting their own negatives or using digital equipment that allows them to go from disk to plate.) As a freelancer, you can pick and choose your market depending on your skill set, once you decide exactly what those skills are.

---

* Both Polaroid and Kodak were slow to notice photography, their main business, was shifting to digital, which requires no film or paper, their main products. Their stocks plummeted and now both companies are in demise. They were a shoo-in to stay on top (because they were family choice, well-known names), had they grasped this. Instead, the market was free for the taking by companies such as Epson, Minolta, and others that exploited the technology wave.

For the first time ever, the web allows you to participate in a global economy without leaving your house. Corporate America (and Canada) has been outsourcing all kinds of jobs overseas for the past decade, with devastating effects on the economy. Asia excels at following in North America's footsteps in industry and production, but falls far behind in original thinking simply because Asian cultures do not encourage independent thought. They encourage conformity, and wherever conformity is the norm, creativity suffers. As a freelancer, you have the potential to make yourself immune from overseas pilfering of jobs no matter what the tax benefits for big business. Although it's easy to learn a new language, learning a culture is another thing entirely. So revel in your abilities to excel in original thinking. It's no accident that the word "free" is a prominent part of "freelance." Remember, "Freedom is a system based on courage."**

2.1 Get high-speed Internet access

One thing that's absolutely necessary to consider if you want to succeed online is a high-speed Internet connection. If you can afford it, it's well worth the money. Large files can be sent online to printers all over the world, and having a broadband connection is preferable to the agony of any dial-up modem connection, no matter how reliable. If cable is not available in your area, look for DSL (Digital Subscriber Line). The price is comparable and the speed is excellent. Should you be so fortunate as to be able to choose between the two, know that cable is faster than DSL and allows more choice as far as how broad the broadband connection is.

What they don't tell you about DSL or cable is that you are always connected. There is no dialing, no waiting for the modem handshake, no inopportune disconnection, and no delay in accessing your email. Boot up your computer and you are online. If your area is limited to dial-up service, as soon as you can afford to, look into a satellite connection (available as a component of DirectTV or from an excellent company called DirecWay) or an ISDN (Integrated Services Digital Network) line from the local phone company. Wireless is preferred for speed and reliability; and may be available in your area.

An ISDN is expensive, but worth the cost if you do a high volume of work online and only have one option. Commit yourself to

** John Bartlett, "Life of Charles Péguy" in *Bartlett's Familiar Quotations* (New York: Little, Brown, 1980).

upgrade your service if need be, as a fast connection will affect your daily business operations and your attitude about working online from this point forward. Whereas you might have been able to make three or four portfolio showings a week in person, online you can ship your portfolio to hundreds of people each week — all over the world.

Like I said, the world is your oyster, but you'll surf faster and happier with a high-speed connection. Even if you live on a 200-acre ranch, DirecWay offers a package deal of cable TV and high-speed Internet for less than $60 per month. The downside is you have to invest $600 in equipment, but you can't beat the speed or the monthly fee for both. Add a Vonage online telephone account and the savings will materialize while you zip along online at un-believable speeds.

A great source for regular work is the government, either local, state or provincial, or federal.

2.2 Design an impressive business website

Do you have your free billboard? That's the way one professional photographer describes his website. Most Internet service providers will allot you 10 megabytes of space for a website as part of your access agreement. (The amount of space varies between providers, so check your contract.) What you get is a lot of space to fill with free advertising. Your website works while you sleep and acts like a beacon, attracting assignments from around the globe 24 hours a day.

Many local community colleges offer low-cost courses in website development. With your creative expertise, such a class might help you learn the basics of HTML coding. If you invest in Adobe's Creative Suite, you'll have everything you need to design your own online portfolio. Your need for a website is also another excellent opportunity for barter if you don't want anything to do with writing code. Find a code writer (aka techie or geek) and trade creative content in exchange for coding your website. If you have time, there are excellent self-help guides for website design online. Some of these resources are listed on the CD included with this book. There are also some special touches called Stupid Web Tricks that may particularly appeal to the creative type.

Invest the time to develop your own corporate identity, and devote time to create an impressive web presence. A word of caution: The whole point of migrating print to the web is accessibility. Whether you dive in and use every fancy design trick the medium allows in presenting your migration is an individual decision. There are about a million sites out there with all sorts of fireworks going off, drawing your undivided attention to *nothing* because there is *no content*. Make sure your website does more than entertain. Remember, the image you create for yourself is just as important as the work you do for a client, so don't throw just anything up online. In fact, the work you do for yourself may be *more* important, because designing a promotion may just determine how successful you are and how quickly you start to earn a living. Extend your creative sense on your own behalf or trade with a peer whose work you admire. Either way, make sure it's a true representation of the quality of work a client might expect if they hired you.

2.3 Make your website searchable

A key element of your website is hidden behind the fancy graphics in source code. No matter what your particular area of creative endeavor, you will need to come up with a list of metatags and keywords. Metatags are source code used by webbots and search engines to find your site and organize it in their information hierarchy. Make a list of every word ever used to describe the skill or service you will offer. Even if you deplore the word "flyer" to describe a direct mail piece, put it in the list. Remember that people doing a Google or Yahoo! search will rely on their own vocabulary to find the service they're looking for online.

Two things determine your rank in the search hierarchy: keywords and links. Keywords tell search engines what you do, and inbound links tell them how important you are. This combination determines your relevance, and relevance is the prime ranking mechanism of search engines. Incorporating keyword phrases into your HTML metatags is only part of what's required. Think of your metatags as arrows. If your metatag keywords aren't used in the copy on the website, your site won't be indexed by those search words. Remember, there's a live person on the other end trolling the Internet, so don't overdo it. Find a balance between copy written for search engines and copy written for real people. After you've got a website, plan on spending some time registering it with various search engines. It usually takes less than 30 days to show up in a search. I recommend paying a listing service to submit your site to various search engines *only* if you are either incredibly rich or incredibly lazy.

2.4 Get up to speed with technology

The first step in effective promotion as a freelancer is preparing your work portfolio for online distribution. This speeds up distribution, enabling you to get the word out quickly that you're open for business. I had an interview with a design studio back when desktop capabilities were just entering the scene. I flipped through my print pieces and launched into my presentation. When I was finished, the client said, "Your work is excellent, but the way you're doing it is so … *antiquated*." Boy, did I feel out of touch. Perhaps she was just alluding to how advanced their staff were as computer users, but her words stung.

As a designer, I was used to being on the cutting edge; and here I was, *antiquated*. I immediately begged, borrowed, and stole any computer time I could to learn what I needed to know. I traded design skills at the local university, volunteering design advice on student publications. Then a friend told me about this guy who bought a computer just so he could say he had a computer. Perfect! I could supply him with a free computer *user*. He didn't know how to use his computer, but he coveted appearing cutting-edge to his clients without going to the trouble of learning how. I started spending mornings in his studio, and when the odd job came in that he needed a comprehensive, I helped out.

Times are different now, and using a computer is mandatory. Most colleges and art schools include computer education as part of the program, and the cost of a good computer has fallen dramatically. Few printers will accept less than digital preparation for output; and as mentioned earlier, if they do, they will charge you for correcting and adjusting your file until it is prepress perfect.

It's no longer practical in today's marketplace to be less than proficient on a computer with updated software. The computer has reduced labor and material costs so much, doing things the old-fashioned way is like using a horse and carriage on the freeway. You *will* get run off the road, and creatives who have the skills will walk away with all your hard-earned business. So you're back to square one if you need computer skills. A quick fix is finding a technically capable student willing to work in exchange for an apprenticeship.

3. Create a Digital Portfolio

Let's return to creating that online portfolio, because it is your talisman. Once limited by the number of hours in a day and how far you could lug your book from place to place, the game of finding work has changed. With the Internet explosion, there are two good ways to quickly get the word out that you are available. Even if you have zero capital to invest, you can get great visibility immediately and for free by either mounting your work on a website or putting together a PDF portfolio.

3.1 Protect Your Work: The Laws of Authorship

One almost famous photographer I know put out a remarkable self-promotion piece. It was a calendar so simple and stunning, everyone wanted one. It was a series of posters with spot varnishes printed in full color on 100-pound coated cover. Being a professional, he stamped a copyright mark on each and every image used to produce those promotional pieces. About six months later, he received a phone call from a printer a thousand miles away. "Say, I've got these stripped up negatives here and I don't see a copyright release. I'll need that before I can proceed with the job." It seems the guy who printed the job for the photographer liked the posters so much, he decided to reprint them quietly out of town for his own promotion, without the knowledge or permission of the photographer. "Hell, no, I'm not giving you my permission." Oh, to be a fly on the wall when those two guys came together.

Having a clear understanding of the differences between copyright, trademark, and patent is important — not only to protect ourselves, but our clients, too. From time to time, forum participants have declared that they have lease agreements with their clients for logos they designed (say what?), that Nike® leases its logo from the designer (aw, go on), that online logo services are restricting some usage rights (the special Frank Zappa "no foolin?"). They want to know how much to increase their design fees if a print run is over or under a certain quantity. They ask what wording is used to transfer certain usage rights when they design a website. None of these questions would be asked if everyone selling design services had a clear understanding of the nature of copyright and fair use. Confusion sets in when one applies the rules of photography or illustration to design. They are very different by definition and one of the steps of registering a creative work is definition. Trust me; if you have trouble defining the parameters of your work as far as ownership, you'll have just as much trouble defining it on all the forms you'll need to file a copyright, trademark, or patent.

When you create a work of art, you are automatically protected by the laws of authorship. Whether a painting, an illustration, a play, or a clay pot, no one can own it but you. Now, if someone buys that item from you, then they own the rights to live with it and display it — but they don't OWN it and may not alter or destroy it. In fact, if they endanger it in any way, the law says it must be restored and returned to the original artist. This applies whether you file any paperwork or not. It's automatic; the only thing you have to do is identify yourself as the artist and that's probably why it's a good idea to sign your work if you are a fine artist.

The difference between fine and commercial art is that very signature: Fine artists put their name on the work, commercial artists get their name on the check. Commercial art involves an assignment from the client which constitutes an understanding that you are designing something specific to that client; custom fees for custom design. Designers who work on the cheap need cheesy schemes to bring in the cash; it's like a Pay-Me-Less tennis shoe store selling shoes for $5 with a per-game usage fee extended for the life of the shoe.

When a photographer shoots a picture, unless he is working under a "work for hire" contract that defines his work product as property of his employer, he owns what he shoots. He may transfer some usage rights or he may sell the thing outright; the difference is the price will rise as the rights increase. When an illustrator receives an assignment from a client, the fee will rise if the illustrator transfers all usage rights to the client, or if he wants to retain some rights so he can sell the illustration again as stock art or if he wants to retain the original. Few clients I know will go to the trouble of hiring an illustrator to do a custom job if they aren't going to be the exclusive owner of the usage rights. That's why illustration is expensive.

When you buy a stock photograph, the agency will ask you how many impressions you will make. If you only need 100 brochures, the stock photo will cost less because you are getting less usage. If your run is over 5 million, you will pay more because more people are seeing the image on behalf of your cause. The risk, which is inherent in figuring the value of a stock photo versus paying for a custom photo shoot, is that you might see the same photo on a competitor's sales piece. Why isn't it the same when you design a brochure? Because you cannot own the elements and their arrangement, and that's all a layout is. After a finite number of people copyrighted their designs, there would be no more design. Who owns text set nine over ten, flush left, rag right, and positioned in the lower left corner of a page? Can't be done.

Copyrighting graphic design would mean someone owned an idea or way of doing things. The trouble, as well as the basis for understanding, comes in the definition of parameters.

Logos are expensive endeavors. Custom anything is more expensive, but when you sit down with a designer and discuss your mission statement, your customer base, your product line and your target market; all of that time figures into the cost of identity development. It would be unethical of a designer to take the product of all that input and resell it later — and that's part of the intrinsic value of a custom logo and why you cannot retain any of the rights. No one is going to hire you to design something that time intensive if they don't end up owning it. Think about it. After the identity is complete and the bill has been paid, the client can register his new logo with the Trademark office; but you cannot copyright it because it was commissioned with the intent of identifying someone else's business.

For writers, newspapers and magazines do not have the right to republish articles written by freelancers in electronic databases without the author's permission, according to a Supreme Court of Canada ruling. The long-running case revolves around Canadian freelance writer Heather Robertson and two articles she wrote to the *Globe and Mail* in 1995. After publication in print, the newspaper put them in three electronic databases without her permission; Info Globe Online, the electronic version of the Canadian Periodical Index (CPI.Q) and a CD that contains a year's worth of several Canadian newspapers. The Ontario Superior Court ruled in favor of Robertson in 2001 and the Ontario Court of Appeals upheld that decision on appeal.

3.2 Put samples of your work on a website

When designing an online portfolio, as with a traditional portfolio, select only your best and most important pieces. Something becomes important when it clearly shows your contribution to the success of the promotion or product. Business places great demands on time, and how you spend yours determines your success in the market-place. Spend your time wisely. Don't stick with the old-fashioned way of showing your work. It may be quaint, but getting the word out quickly is more important than personal visits. When someone does ask for an appointment, appreciate it and be respectful of his time. Once you've selected work that best shows off your talents, work on presenting it as a website. But be prepared to present a hard copy when you meet a cyber-illiterate client. This person may have a computer on his desk, but it is strictly for show. These are usually established executives close to retirement who rely on their secretarial staff to pump out documents for their review. If they ever want to actually see your work, it will be in printed form.

Remember that whatever you put online is open to thievery and debauchery of the worst kind. The average person is unaware of how wrong it is to steal somebody else's work and use it for themselves. Sometimes, those who appropriate others' work don't have a creative bone in their bodies. Noncreative people have little idea of what's involved in creating something and just don't know "adopting" is wrong. This was demonstrated to me — once again — just recently.

A building manufacturer hired me to put together a brochure. He was just starting out and had no finished projects to photograph. The obvious solution was to build a few installations for his parents and siblings, or even for a local charity. Then he would not only get good examples of his work, but maybe some free publicity from the local charity. Instead, this client directed me to websites belonging to his competition and told me to download photography to use in his brochure. I informed him politely that this was illegal and punishable at $75,000 per offense. He said, "Uh, oh, really?" I was pegged again as uncooperative, and he took his brochure elsewhere.

Laws exist to protect creatives from being victimized in this way. Let's take a quick detour to review copyright law.

3.2a What's yours to put in your portfolio?

What can you legally put in your portfolio? Very often, the work you do while you are employed by someone else may seem like their property. It is not; it is a sample of your creativity and talent and may be shown with or without their approval and permission as long as you do not contact their clients. The courts have ruled in noncompete cases that an artist's portfolio is the same as a resume; it is a visual record of your work history and no one has a right to restrict your use of that in a free enterprise system. Therefore, everything you do is game for your portfolio, big or small. Don't fall for the threats, demands, or petty vindictiveness that may ensue when you use a particularly nice piece and previous employers try to put up a fight. They have no ground to stand on unless you intentionally call on their clients. That's called tortuous interference because you are disrupting an established business relationship and that is against the law.

My website (a.k.a. digital portfolio) contains a website I designed while I was an employee. I received an email from the new owners of the business, demanding that I remove that website from my portfolio.

If you know the rules, it's easy to respond to such a demand without worry. Here's my response to the new manager:

"That website is part of my design portfolio which is used in the same way you might use a résumé under the law. But I will have my webmaster insert a line of text that prohibits search engines from finding it. Feel free to correspond directly with me if you have any other issues."

Most demands will cease and desist, as this one did, once they realize you know your rights under the law.

3.2b US Copyright

You do not need to file a copyright registration application to get copyright protection, nor do you need to use a copyright notice. If you create a painting, sell it, and discover it's been altered by an overly enthusiastic interior designer without your permission, you can rescue your painting and sue for damages and restoration costs.

The original copyright act was passed in 1909. Congress passed the Copyright Revision Act of 1976 to extend the period of protection. The revised copyright law gave federal protection —

- for the life of the creator plus 50 years if the creator is a human being and the work was not a work made for hire; or

- if the creator is a hypothetical person, such as a corporation, or if the work is created under a pseudonym or published anonymously, then the period of protection is either 100 years from creation or 75 years from the date of first publication, whichever period expires first.

On October 27, 1998, President Clinton signed into law the Sonny Bono Copyright Term Extension Act, which extended the terms of almost all existing copyrights by 20 years. The basic term of copyright protection, the life of the creator plus 50 years, has been increased to life plus 100 years. The most recent law passed was the Online Copyright Infringement Liability Limitation Act, which extended copyright protection to digital art, too.

3.2c Canadian Copyright

If you are a Canadian, your work is protected from theft or alteration during the course of your lifetime plus the remainder of the calendar year in which you die, and for 50 years following your death. After that, your work will become part of the public domain.

You do not need to apply for copyright protection because in Canada, you are covered as soon as the work is produced. Note that an idea for a novel is not copyrightable, but the completed manuscript is.

If you sell your copyrighted work to someone else, you still keep what are called "moral rights" of the work. Moral rights protect your work from being distorted, mutilated, or otherwise modified in a way that is harmful to your honor or reputation. Even the new copyright owner cannot infringe on your moral rights without your permission. Moral rights exist for the same length of time as copyright (i.e., your lifetime plus 50 years).

For more information on copyright laws in Canada go to the Department of Justice's website at http://laws.justice.gc.ca.

So rest easy that what you create is yours alone (except under certain circumstances covered in Chapter 11). It's best to avoid dealing with unscrupulous clients; they are not worth the grief.

3.3 Create a PDF portfolio

There is a much faster, more personal way to show your work to the right people, beyond posting it on a website. It isn't as personal as making an appointment in person, but it certainly increases the number of contacts with potential customers you can make in a very short time. Actually, in some ways, it's far more intimate than a personal visit. If your website is still "under construction," create a PDF portfolio that you can send as an attachment with emails. This will come in handy while you refine your website. As soon as your website is available, include an active link in your email instead of sending the PDF. It won't take as long to download and your potential client can simply click on the link instead of launching Adobe Reader and opening your PDF file.

To create a close-ended file that viruses and malicious macros won't attach to, you'll need a program capable of exporting files in Portable Document Format (PDF). Using a program such as Adobe InDesign, Adobe PageMaker, QuarkXPress, or Macromedia FreeHand, create a file that contains your digital portfolio. Design this file knowing it will be viewed privately at the time of the client's time of choosing. If you are a writer, this is an excellent opportunity to barter with a designer.

The same rules apply to assembling this portfolio as the one you show in person or put on your website: don't make it too big and be sure to make it interesting. You'll need to include some text (since you won't be on hand to explain each piece) and a short bio at the end of the file. You can also include the highlights of your résumé, as long as you keep these concise. Add your logo and make sure this file is as excellent as your work. Then export it as a screen version PDF. Before you send it out, do some serious research online to decide the target companies you want to contact and who the appropriate person is at each firm.

3.3a   Send an introductory email

If you have a copywriter among your friends — and what professional designer doesn't know a few writers — ask him to write a letter of introduction for you. This, too, is an excellent opportunity to barter. Briefly list your experience, your website link if it's available, and any client websites you'd like the recipient to visit. Put all of this in a draft file and save it in the drafts folder of your email program.

As you change targets, edit your letter so that it relates to the industry you're targeting. Be sure to add tidbits of information that qualify you to work in that particular industry. Mention that you are attaching your PDF portfolio file to the email because your website is under construction, if that is the case. Because not everybody is technically savvy, tell the potential client the file can be opened with Adobe Reader. This miracle software package is free and inherent on almost every computer, whether it's a PC or a Macintosh. It can also be downloaded at no charge at many sites online.

3.3b   Make sure the recipient has adequate IP service

A word of caution: Before you attach your PDF, make sure the recipients don't have slow dial-up service. (Their email addresses will sometimes tip you off.) If they do, they will never see your portfolio, since some service providers, such as America Online (AOL), frequently delete attachments to limit available bandwidth.

Most companies realize the importance of a good service provider. When you see an amateur's service provider, it's a dead giveaway the company has no money to spend or doesn't see the Internet as an instrument of commerce. This is not likely a client who will be able to justify the expense of hiring a professional. Don't waste your time or theirs chasing after a paper airplane when there are a lot of private jets out there.

3.3c   Always thank the recipients for their time

Always practice the age-old cardinal rule of business: Remember to thank recipients of your email for their time. Time is the one thing everybody gets to spend only once. So don't waste any of your time *or theirs*. Make a quick entry and exit; don't sit around making small talk unless you're encouraged to. Get to the point and acknowledge the time expenditure the potential client made on your behalf to help you inform him of your service.

3.3d   Attach a compelling JPEG sample

One last tip to ensure email visibility: Include a small, dramatic piece of work in JPEG format. I use a particularly well-known logo, but a catchy quote is just as effective. (Okay, visual creatives do have the advantage.) Most email programs automatically display JPEGS in the window of the email message. If your JPEG selection is compelling, your target will know two things:

1.   You are not wasting their time.

2.   Your work is of a certain caliber.

These are two very important qualifying markers for a prospective client.

3.3e   Use online directories to target clients

Cold calling potential clients this way is easier than you think. Once you have your letter and PDF file ready, the fishbowl becomes a farm. Get yourself a big glass of iced tea and sit down at the computer to show your work to the world. In what industry or service area would you like to work? Find it with your favorite search engine and work the directory of choice. My background in medical products made surgical products and medical equipment an obvious choice. An online directory of suppliers showed me at least a hundred potential clients.

If you feel a bit shy about cold calling, start out in a familiar area. This can bolster your spirit and build your courage. Great feedback helps, too, and all it takes is one or two favorable responses to keep at it. Targeting your market online takes time, but nowhere near the time it takes to physically transport your book from place to place. Click on the link and go to the company website. Look for a person to direct your inquiry to — preferably someone who clearly has something to do with the type of work you're looking for.

Websites vary in content, and sometimes they provide a full roster of employees so you can direct your email to exactly the right person. If that information is not available, don't hesitate to use the general mailbox at the website. Nine times out of ten, you can rely on the good graces of the webmaster. Chances are, they may delete your pitch, but more often than not, they will forward it to the right person. I've gotten more clients from using the subject line, "Please direct to the right person/thanks!" than I ever got from knowing the right person's name. So don't fall into the trap of thinking it won't work. It does work — and more often than you'd expect. By using the information on strategic alliances in the next chapter and employing the directory listings of your favorite search engine, you will soon have more contacts than time.

3.3f   Go where the work is — without leaving home

Learn to use the hundreds of online directories to your advantage. In an economic downturn, market yourself to industries that are successful. When oil and gas are depressed, market yourself to hospitals — go where the paying customers are. Be smart in how you invest your time. In former days, when appointments and handshakes were necessary and it took all week to show your portfolio to five people, cold calling was a real chore. Sometimes, after all that work, you still didn't find work.

With online cold calling, you never leave the comfort of your home office. You can send your PDF portfolio all over the world, and before you know it, the phone will start ringing and your bank account will grow. Actually, I have several clients I've never spoken to on the phone. They send me emails and I respond. Some of the writers I work with, thousands of miles away, don't miss the nagging ring of the phone at all. They send me text files and I design. If you think green, there's no better way to save energy or a few trees; and it's not bad missing out on that long-distance telephone bill.

Cold calling online has many advantages besides saving on gas and wear and tear on shoe leather. It gives your prospect the option of not being interested without using up your resources. I drove more than 60 miles (95 kilometers) to show my work to one prospective client. When I arrived at the studio, the principal was busy with a client and refused to look at my work. Online, if they aren't interested, you'll never hear from them, and you won't have to spend money or time to find it out.

3.3g Hook your client with the perfect subject line

You can make that email subject line work to your advantage by inventing a hook. Write the perfect line that creates curiosity in your target. What can you put on that subject line that creates interest but doesn't tell the whole story? What tension can you create that will compel the reader to read and forward your message? Sometimes a simple approach works best, as the following example shows.

When I was contacting scientists and doctors who might need design work in creating compliance sheets and documentation for online dissemination in PDF format, my hook was "RE: your scientific & financial documents." Why is that a hook? Most companies are looking for investors; just in case this message is from an investor, my recipient's desire will compel him to *read* instead of *delete*. If my target thinks the message is from a government agency requesting backup documentation for his research, again, chances are the message will be read. Advertising is about motivating people emotionally to do what needs to be done. In this instance, it is not deceptive to play on a person's assumptions and predispositions if the end result is he realizes he can use your services. It's a competitive world out there, and if you want clients' attention, you have to work for it.

3.3h Follow up with interested prospects

When people are interested, they will respond and query you about your rates and turnaround times. Remember to keep an email address book and periodically contact the people who have responded positively. Now and then, send them an email with a JPEG attachment of work recently completed to keep in touch. Do the same prior to holidays, sending something eye-catching that goes with the holiday spirit.

Whatever you decide to send, make sure it represents your best work. Though it's true in advertising that all publicity is good publicity, there is one exception to this rule. J. Lo can change her hairstyle and make you forget her last boyfriend, but a bad piece of work sticks in a client or potential client's memory like a rotten egg. You can be sure that after living with it for however long it takes to use up those 30,000 print copies, that particular client will remember the bad taste it left in his mouth and won't be calling again.

4. Register for Government Contracts

Here's a tip especially for those of you who don't have spectacular portfolios. A great source for regular work is the government, either local, state or provincial, or federal. There are a series of steps you should take to make the process less painful.

Note that government work is fraught with contracts and much paperwork, so be forewarned. If you the think the fishbowl is challenging, this milieu is a sea of paperwork with a long wait for payment after the work is done unless you accept government credit cards (approved for all purposes less than $2,500 in the US only). Registering at the following sites is a quick way to get the word out to hundreds of thousands of government employees that you are available, so it's never a waste of time. The downside is you may spend a month registering everywhere and never get a single job. The upside is you may be selected as a single source contractor for a five-year contract with some nationwide government agency, and all of their work will be directed to you. Is registering worth your time? Only you know the answer.

4.1 US government contracts

In the US, the first step for registering for a government contract is to get a DUNS number. You can't even begin the registration process without that number, so use the few days it takes to be assigned your business number to gather up leads and resources.

You'll need to search for a set of numbers the government uses to catalog the type of service or product you provide. This series of numbers is called the NAICS Industry Group. You may choose to list your service in many different categories, so take the time to list in more than one area. Another good starting point is the Small Business Administration (SBA) website, www.sba.gov, which will guide you through the process, producing some valuable leads and highly effective contacts.

When you register with the Central Contractors Register (CCR), your name will pop up every time a government agency is looking for the creative service you sell. Keep this information updated, because it is the main search area for government employees looking for suppliers and sources. Once you complete all the online forms, register at various corporate sites that are a good source of subcontracting work, such as Martin-Marrietta and Raytheon. If you meet all the various criteria, big government contractors will be able to select you as a prime subcontractor for specialized services. However, if you list yourself in the wrong category, don't be surprised if you start getting requests for quotes on supplying a hundred thousand pairs of pink jockey shorts to a prison in Idaho.

You can further increase your chances of getting work by qualifying as a minority-owned, woman-owned, or veteran-owned small business or a business in a HUBZone (Historically Underutilized Business Zone). There are set-asides for businesses that pass certification with the SBA, and such certification will increase your chances of getting government projects even if your bid is high. Many people interested in government work try to pass the stringent requirements for getting listed on the General Services Administration (GSA) list of approved vendors, but the last time I checked, the application was 200 pages long and required a $125 processing fee. After you do all this paperwork, pay the money, and meet the stringent requirements, there's still no guarantee you'll ever get a contract. Even in this arena, the best way to get work is to provide excellent service at a competitive price.

Set a schedule to tackle the many opportunities out there with major corporations that have large diversity programs designed to help small businesses grow. Sometimes you have to register with each corporation in addition to registering at the government websites. Give it a shot and see what happens. You may end up handling all the print for the next presidential campaign. You never know.

4.2 Canadian government contracts

A great source for regular government work in Canada is the Government Electronic Tendering system (MERX). You can subscribe to MERX on an annual basis or pay to download a specific Request for Proposal (RFP). MERX provides their subscribers access to many opportunities with the federal government, participating provincial governments, municipal governments, and from the private sector. Note that MERX is used generally for higher-dollar value contracts. For more information, go to their website at www.merx.com.

For lower-dollar value contracts, go to the government's Contracts Canada website at contractscanada.gc.ca, where you can register in the Supplier Registration Information (SRI) service as a potential supplier to the government of Canada. Remember to keep your account information updated because once you register, you are a part of a directory of vendors that Public Works and Government Services Canada (PWGSC) consults for suppliers and sources. If your account goes out of date with an incorrect ad 'ress or other wrong information, you may miss out on good jobs.

If you are a supplier wanting to do business with the federal government, go to Contracts Canada's website to understand how the government does its buying.

Chapter **6**

STRATEGIC ALLIANCES

At one time, almost everything that was written and designed was slated for print. Now, less than half will be produced in print. That's a major change in the market, and with the expansion of online marketing, many companies no longer invest in print publications at all. In a recent poll, 47 percent of printers said their business was poor or not as good as it was four years ago, and 9 percent of those said their business was very bad.* At the same time, printers cited the challenge of replacing jobs lost to Internet or PDF nonprint publishing as their least important concern.

To these printers I would say, "Wake up!" If you think the printing industry is depressed now, get ready to see a major slide in production as more businesses discover the beauty of transferring the cost of output to the end user. Although the survey takers noted a small rise in concern in the industry, this is the next big hit the graphic arts will take in the coming decade. Those businesses who once provided the bread-and-butter work for printers are realizing the power of Portable Document Format (PDF). They want to feel the impact on their bottom lines of transferring printing costs to the user — and they will, once they provide all documentation online.

---

* CAP Ventures, Inc., *The New Corporate Print Customer: A Profile of a Market in Transition* (independent study, 2004), 46. The full report is available at InfoTrends/CAP Ventures www.capv.com/home/Multiclient/newcorporateprint.html.

Whether material is printed or used as an online download, clients will always need writers and designers.

Remember when typesetting was replaced by desktop publishing? Get ready for the next technology shift. The rage in sales literature and product brochures is the same PDF file type I recommend for your portfolio. What used to be mandatory from a designer's perspective in annual reports (fine paper, excellent photography) has been reconstituted as a PDF for public consumption. (No more fine art printing, fine paper stock, or high-end photography, because all three are defeated by the end user's printer quality.) Paper companies are closing plants left and right, sometimes to avoid compliance with new environmental regulations but more often to consolidate operation expenditures. Though it has taken a while to happen, we really are moving toward a paperless society. That's great news for the forests, but not so great if you are in printing or paper sales.

But rest easy if you're a creative professional, because whether material is printed or used as an online download, clients will always need writers and designers. According to a study conducted by CAP Ventures, Inc., corporations on average spend approximately 3 percent of their total revenue on print with outside vendors. As a freelance designer, you are a prime outside source for this work. The same study revealed that almost two-thirds of participants transmit information electronically, and they expect this trend to grow significantly.* This means many creatives are easily downloading text files and photography online from customers who buy freelance creative services. Your life as a freelancer has never been easier.

The CAP Ventures study also revealed that approximately one-third of the corporations surveyed currently use variable information printing — they no longer rely on slick paper and printers to create their sales literature. Even though these companies rely on Print-on-Demand (POD) technology, obsolete documents are still an issue. On average, 12.6 percent of print becomes obsolete before it can be used.* The companies surveyed cited printing, delivery costs, and document accuracy as their most significant problems. These problems will push industry to rely more on PDF technology and do less actual production. There will be more work for designers and less work for paper houses and printers. Now's the time to get comfortable with PDF technology and start selling it to your clients as a viable alternative to big-budget, slick brochures. If you own printing equipment, start looking for a buyer before the market is flooded with equipment.

---

* CAP Ventures, 46–47.

1. PDF — How It Reconfigured Sales Support

Let's talk about Portable Document Format (PDF) in more detail. This revolutionary file format allows anyone at any level to open a file you've created, using Adobe Reader. This software is installed on most computers and is available for free download at various online sites. Previously, if you wanted to send a client or friend a copy of something you had designed, you had to make sure they had their monitor set to millions of colors. Then you had to be sure they had all the right fonts and the right program to open the file. Few people have all the necessary components.

In contrast, documents saved as PDFs can be opened on any computer and display exactly as you created them. This makes proofing possible from one side of the country to the other. It makes client approval fast and accurate and really reduces preparation time. No more glossy paper comprehensives mounted and shipped out for approval, only to arrive dog-eared. No more long meetings in the conference room, waiting for the client to decide on various adjustments and changes. With PDFs, you can continue working while your clients review your work in the privacy of their offices. If they have questions, they can simply phone you. For the first time, you no longer need to take half a day and drive to a meeting with a client to show them the final proof.

Most design programs, such as Adobe PageMaker, Adobe InDesign, Quark-XPress, and Macromedia FreeHand, have export functions under the file menu that allow you to export the document you just created as a PDF file. A word of caution: Be sure to save your document before you export; some programs do an automatic save before creating the PDF. You cannot delete a few things, do an export, and expect to revert to the unsaved, unaltered document. Another thing to keep in mind: PostScript is native to Adobe products, but not to Quark. (Read more about this issue in section **2.6** of Chapter 2.) Aside from the major cost-cutting advantage, the PDF transfers the cost of printing from the company to the user. All the money previously spent on fine paper and four-color printing is being tucked away in employee pension plans. Gone are the budget restrictions limiting the number of colors and the photography; now, the sky's the limit. But this also means you have to consider the end product when designing for PDF output, as all that control you had over paper stock and ink spread will disappear. Your beautiful brochure might be printed on 20-pound white bond or whatever neon color Junior left in the family printer.

The other immediate advantage to business is there's no more postage, packaging, or delay in getting sales support to a target market. Just like impulse buying at the grocery counter, our passion for immediate gratification works online for big business when they employ a POD brochure. That sudden "just-gotta-have-it" urge will push customers to buy as soon as decision-making information is in their hands. A PDF prevents delay; without a cooling-off period, consumers will act quickly to relieve that emotional tension and buy. I already touched on how the PDF also frees up creatives. Without budget restriction, your client can do a seven-color brochure because he will never be stuck paying for make-ready on a four-color printing press. The only fee that remains constant is your fee — the talent. This works out well for a whole generation of desktop publishers and folks who traverse the shady line between advertising and journalism — that gray area of working professionals who know little about production requirements and frequently find themselves short on technical specifications. PDF publications designed strictly for online download will keep less knowledgeable designers out of the alligator pit, but still allow them to please their clients and make a living.

2. Opportunities for Strategic Alliances

Because of this change in the marketplace, new alliances can be made that benefit everybody. When I first started out, one of the printers I used for some small jobs took it upon himself to direct work to me. He ran a large print shop in a big city, and though I was too ignorant to appreciate it, he took me under his wing. I forgot about those ten other designers and thought, in all naïveté, that he used me because he needed me. What he was doing was throwing work my way to keep me from starving to death. Quite by accident, I took all the design work I did back to him, but I suspect at this late date that he knew I would.

This type of partnership works well for both parties. If you're new on the scene and need a way to get business, introducing yourself to a local printer usually nets a few jobs right away if he or she likes your work. Bear in mind that printers are sticklers for perfection; if your production skills are poor or you have a tendency to blow your nose on your cover sheets, don't look to your printer to call you back.

They quoted one job and I thought I was protected because I stipulated all changes and alterations as part of a flat fee on the bid sheet. My client was well known for making last-minute revisions without consideration for deadlines or cost, and I had to protect the company from itself on this typesetting job. The type house was aware of the bad habits and late changes. The owner of the type house sent the bill when the job was complete and it was as quoted, much to my surprise. About a month later, the owner sold his company. Within a week, I received a bill for the job's revisions from the new owner, twice the original quote! The previous owner had pulled a fast one on the new buyer, showing a dollar amount for revisions as uncollected. After they reviewed the written quote at my urging, it became clear that it was not money owed, but a clever circumvention of due diligence.

Enter their new salesman, Clark Kent, sent over to mend fences and try for new business. He persevered and worked on me until I finally gave him another chance. Eventually, he became my typesetter of choice and did all my work. When he made a career change to print salesman, again, he did all my work. His perseverance paid off and it can pay off for you, too.

Chapter 7

COLD CALLING FOR NEW BUSINESS

The hardest part of starting a new business is believing there will be more work when you finish whatever you're working on now. One professional photographer I know spends a lot of time wringing his hands and sweating about where the next job is coming from — and he's been self-employed for more than 20 years, or, as he calls it, "nearly unemployed." You might as well stop worrying right now and trust that everything will fall into place if you do the work to make it so. Spend your time following up leads and leave the worrying to the cat.

Cold calling is every salesman's nightmare. There's nothing worse than being greeted like a door-to-door salesman, and that's exactly how cold calling got its name. Nevertheless, promise yourself early on that you will dedicate a certain amount of time to finding new business each week, no matter how much work you have. Clients move on for various reasons, and it's nice to have a new one ready when the old one leaves.

Remember that you're not selling widgets. Your product or service is unique and, depending on your work, you may be the only one capable of producing this particular style. Since you determined your unique product when you first started down this road, how you emphasize this skill will determine how easily you find work.

Build your confidence and strike out with your work.

Consider it a disservice to humanity if you keep your wonderful talents to yourself. With that attitude, potential clients will be unable to resist their curiosity and your sales pitch.

The wildest cold call I ever made was when I worked up a complete set of color comprehensives, mounted them on black board, and shipped them off with a letter of introduction to the owner of a big company in a distant city. The owner loved my work and invited me to show my portfolio. I drove the distance once and cemented our working relationship, and was rewarded with a steady flow of work for the next few years, until the company was sold. Build your confidence and strike out with your work. You can't win the lottery if you don't buy a ticket. Here are some other pointers for drumming up new business.

1. Defrosting Those Icy Cold Calls

"Hello. Is there anyone in particular I might show my portfolio? I'm freelance." This was my opener when calling a large agency where chances of showing my work were slim to none. Inevitably, the person answering the phone was taken aback that I did not seek to hide my purpose or intent; plus I was asking for their help in reaching the right person. Ad agencies will frequently assign portfolio reviews to one art director who will either let you pass go or dismiss you with a handshake, so it's not always possible to research the facts. Getting your work out in front of the hiring public is a task you will face for most of your professional life, and the cold call is a key point to master. For some folks, making a cold call is possibly the worst feeling in the world. They are, after all, risking immediate rejection and that hurts. It shouldn't hurt, though, because the basis for rejection is nothing personal — they don't know enough about you to make it personal. Keep that in mind and fear will fly out the window.

My second tip for making a cold call less painful is what I call the 50/50 Save. Everything is a 50/50 proposition; the results of your cold call will either be yes or no in all of their various shades of gray. That means there's a 50/50 chance you'll get to show your book, a 50/50 chance you'll land a new client, a 50/50 chance they'll keep you in mind for the next job. They will or they won't and that largely depends on the quality of your work. For me, cold calls have resulted in some long time friendships that keep me growing both professionally and personally. The added option to those cold calls: you, too, may make valuable friends.

Some friends in the business were slow to take to cyberlife. I, on the other hand, was smacked in the face by another friend I cold called in the eighties. My friend Dennis was the guy who took care of a local job board, so I had to call him when I was looking for a job. When computers took over the industry, he told me to, "Get on the computer or take up flipping burgers for a living because you'll be out of a job." I took his advice and always listen when he speaks, er ... emails. My other cold call friend was the creative director at a pretty famous business-to-business (B2B) ad agency in Houston. I called him up and asked if he would he give me some pointers on my work. I had been freelancing for four years when I showed my book, mostly for small businesses that barely had budgets. He taught me the importance of doing a good job instead of appeasing an uneducated client. I would've missed both of these friendships had I not made those cold calls.

My third tip for cold calls is to reframe your mental perspective. Business books say set a couple of hours aside each week to make cold calls. If it was that simple, fewer books would be written about it and more people would be doing it. I get a feeling of dread whenever I have to do something I don't want to; unless I can reframe it for my creative mind. I do one of two things when faced with cold calls. I remind myself that I am selling an original style of work that is uniquely my own; and even if they don't have an assignment for me at this moment, if they are smart, they will take this opportunity to view my work — keeping it in mind for future needs. That's a double whammy because if they don't want to see my work, it means they're not thinking ahead. And who wants to work with short-sighted people, eh? If you're good, they missed more than you did.

The second reframing technique is to escape my dread for whatever chore is at hand. At the first sign of dread, doing almost anything else is more desirable. That, I find, is the most opportune moment to make a cold call. Facing the unknown to avoid drudgery turns the cold call into sheer adventure (and temporary escape from the drudgery). After all, it costs you nothing and you risk nothing. Most important, remember you gain nothing if you don't try. Don't want to clean your studio? Why not make a couple of phone calls to complete strangers?

It's bound to be more fun than cleaning the house.

2. Get to Know Your Competition

Let's say you just dropped out of the sky. How would you start to earn a living? First, get out there and introduce yourself to the competition. Meet the printers, design studios, and ad agencies so they know their competition. Keep in mind that the right chemistry might result in getting some overflow work. Present yourself as a friendly peer instead of the competition and build camaraderie. Make a point of showing your book to illustration studios and T-shirt shops, too, as you never know when one of their clients will ask for a referral. You have lower overhead and a bit of hunger working on your side, plus client accessibility, so make your best effort to attract their business. Be grateful for competitors' time, their opinions of your work, and any advice they may give you.

Keep in mind that some competitors may try to dissuade you from pursuing new business, because it's a small fishbowl and they aren't particularly interested in sharing the work. In a small market, this attitude is more prevalent than you might realize. I moved to a rural area and was met with serious hostility from the local printer. There were no local designers and he had enjoyed a captive market for many years. Of course he wasn't happy to see me; my work was better than his, and I might move the area's printing to a new supplier.

One group of professional women had the same logo as everyone else in the area — an outline of the state with some black type in it. The local printer "designed" those logos, and that's why they all looked miserably alike. I designed a new corporate identity for the company and included letterhead, a business envelope, and business cards. They took it to the local printer, who took more than a month to print 2,000 sheets. He was running their three-color design on a single-color press and struggled to register the colors because he was too stubborn to put the work on a bigger press.

Some time later, I stopped by to introduce myself. I knew staff at the print shop would recognize the logo I had designed, which is usually a good thing. Boy, did they ever. "*That* was a real bitch to print," said the printer's wife. My retort, "It wasn't designed to be printed with potatoes, silly," went unsaid. I left my business card in good faith but decided they weren't interested in partnering. If this happens to you, just think of Dionne Warwick singing "Walk On By," and walk on by to the next opportunity.

3. Avoid Naysayers at All Costs

People can be very protective of their business and sometimes forget that everyone is entitled to make a living. Don't let a bad attitude get you down. For every naysayer out there, you'll find ten others who meet you with enthusiasm and support. Probably some of your competition started out freelancing, so if you can touch their hearts by mentioning you're just starting out, you'll get farther faster. An entrepreneur is more likely to give you a chance to show your skills if given the opportunity. After all, someone gave him his first break. Don't be timid about cold-calling your competition; you might find a mentor who will come in handy when you need advice. Most printers greet a new designer as another spice on their rack, as each new style is an alternative selection for their roster of clients.

This should be particularly true for an illustration studio. I once interviewed for a full-time job with a well-known illustrator in a major metropolitan area. The first thing I did was look through the portfolio in his lobby. It was filled with ads that had a big illustration either at the top or to one side, with a little bit of copy next to the picture. It was easy to tell he had no training in advertising design, and I thought this made my talents a nice complement to his skill set. There were stunning watercolor illustrations framed in the lobby, all signed by his last name, and it looked like this would be a great opportunity to learn from a master. Boy, was I ever wrong.

I took the job and found out later that the fabulous illustrations were by his famous brother, not the man I worked for. The latter was insecure, unhappy, and did things like throw his airbrush against the wall when it clogged. He babbled on about how he didn't have the luxury of an education, that he was the only real artist left in town. When you are a creative person, negative people are counterproductive, and you should steer clear of them whenever possible. Watch out for phrases such as "It can't be done" and "It will never work." Most successful freelancers work to maintain a positive attitude; if you wallow in self-doubt and uncertainty, prospective clients will pick up on this and read it as professional inadequacy instead of what it really is — a little personal doubt coupled with some fear of the unknown.

4. Know the Many Meanings of No

Cold-calling, like advertising, has a few limitations. On hearing the word no, you have to resist emotionally withdrawing, sinking into

Set limits for what you will endure and accept under the guise of getting work.

sadness, and gathering up your samples in an effort to make a mad dash for the door. Like developing a thick skin to jeers on the playground, you have to develop an internal optimism and say something like "Even so, I hope you'll remember my work and know I'm eager and available to help out" while at the same time you may be saying to yourself, "This has been a real waste of time."

Try to remember that sometimes no means *not now*. Your frame of mind should be that you offer a viable service your potential customer might need one day, and you are doing them a favor by informing them of your availability. When you're cold calling, you do have to mind your manners and respect the client's no. The very action of resisting, ignoring the no, may be read as unwillingness to cooperate later on a job. *No* comes in many forms. Sometimes it's "I'm never going to need your services," and this is a person who is overwhelmed, so leave a card and perhaps a promotional piece with your website address. It is always worth the time to check back later in the month to see if they have time to view your work. Last but not least, remember to ask for their email address. If nothing else, let your work speak for you: send them your PDF portfolio or the URL for your website. Sometimes no means just that; the person is married to a creative or they secretly wish they were creative and impose their limited skill on company publications; or, finally, there just isn't a budget. There are many reasons someone may not want to let you introduce yourself. Develop a good sense of when things truly are a waste of your time and theirs. Don't take it personally and above all else, know when to withdraw your efforts.

5. Show Respect and Expect It in Return

Finally, never just show up or drop in unannounced. This not only shows a real disrespect for the other person's time, but also reflects badly on your sense of self-importance. Always call to make an appointment the week before you want to show your book. And with the nature of our business, it's common courtesy to call again early on the day of your appointment to make sure your potential client is still available. Health problems, weather, production delays, last-minute scheduling conflicts: These are things that may make your appointment impractical. Calling the day of the appointment gives both parties a chance to verify availability. If you don't, you may find yourself waiting in the lobby while your client is off doing an impromptu press check.

The reverse also applies: Besides showing respect, you should expect to receive it. If you find your host disinterested or rude during your portfolio showing, you can be sure he or she will be that way during assignments as well. Sometimes vying for business isn't worth the trouble, and it's time to go.

One department head at a major university had a bad habit of accumulating an audience. It didn't matter to her that certain members of the audience in her office had prescheduled appointments. She was performing, and the more the merrier. She loved people and surrounded herself with staff and visitors, both invited and uninvited. During my portfolio showing for contract work, she took phone calls, signed off on documents, asked for coffee, and even left the room a couple of times to meet a tour group. After an hour of this, I made my excuses and headed for the door.

People talk a lot about respecting the boundaries of business, but it's up to you to demand respect for your own boundaries. Set limits for what you will endure and accept under the guise of getting work. Pursue business only with people you like. As I mentioned before, creativity emanates from the same side of your brain as your emotions, and being unhappy will affect your work. Be happy and your work will show it.

6. See the Potential in Every Contact

Let's reiterate a few important points. Cold calling is aptly named; there's nothing pleasant about it, especially for creative people who enjoy their solitude. Keep an open mind and remember that no contact is ever wasted, no matter how far-fetched you might think it is when you try. I wrote a letter to an editor once at a nationwide publication and freely shared a few of my ideas on improving her magazine's appeal to young women. I was 19 years old and shared some ideas about improving photography and layout. About two weeks later, the publisher called me and asked me to fly out for an interview as Director of Advertising.

Another opportunity presented itself when I read a newspaper column written by a guy who had a cartoon strip. He was lamenting that his recent divorce had left his walls blank because his ex-wife had absconded with both the furniture and the artwork. So I sent him a poster I was handing out at the time; I mean, nobody should have blank walls. He called me up and asked me if I was interested in doing the brushwork for his strip. Unfortunately, my brushwork in art school was compared to painting with a mop, so I declined. But it was a worthwhile contact that led to some freelance assignments a few years later.

When you've had a few too many negative responses and feel your feet dragging and your enthusiasm waning, remember the words of a wise man named Calvin Coolidge. President Coolidge addressed the agents of the New York Life Insurance Company in 1932, a few years after the stock market had crashed and when the country was deep in depression. The market for insurance had evaporated, as most people were struggling to keep food on the table and a roof over their heads today, without much vision to insure tomorrow.

> *Nothing in the World can take the place of persistence. Talent will not; nothing is more common than unsuccessful men with talent. Genius will not; unrewarded genius is almost a proverb. Education will not; the world is full of educated derelicts. Persistence and determination alone are omnipotent. The slogan "press on" has solved and will always solve the problems of the human race.**

So press on, persevere, and get that portfolio and your particular skill set exposed to the world.

---

* This quote by Coolidge (1872 –1933) is unverified, but appeared on the cover of a memorial program for him in 1933. From *Respectfully Quoted: A Dictionary of Quotations Requested from the Congressional Research Service*, edited by Suzy Platt (Washington, D.C.: Library of Congress, 1989), quote number 1355 on Bartleby.com, www.bartleby.com/73/1355.html.

Chapter 8

NEGOTIATING WITH VENDORS

No matter what your creative input on a project, handing it off to another person to produce is a scary proposition. When you hand off responsibility for production results, you are relinquishing responsibility for your reputation. Watch out for clients who want to handle their own printing, because no matter what they end up with, you get the credit (or discredit, as the case may be). It's not fair and it's not right, but whatever goes wrong will be blamed on you.

You don't really think the printer will accept responsibility for poor coverage in a solid that should have been designed to accommodate the printing press? Nah, he told the client "the designer knows solids need to run vertically on that kind of press." And you certainly don't think your client is going to take responsibility for signing off on a bad color match, do you? Trust me, there are more bad designers than there are birds in the sky when clients handle their own printing.

Whatever you create during the course of your career stands as a hallmark to your standards, so remember the first rule of freelancing: Always handle the printing for your designs unless the work is for an ad agency with a knowledgeable production manager or someone else you can trust.

Make sure the quality of your printer's work reflects favorably on you and your future.

1. Choose a Reputable Printer

Select vendors who will do an excellent job of producing your work before the negotiations begin. To find them, use word of mouth, or research a print piece by tracing its source to figure out exactly who does quality work. It's a good idea to note a printer's work when you make the rounds of printers looking for assignments. You can be sure the printer is gauging you according to your work, so return the favor.

If you've ever had a typo in a print piece, you know how you feel every time you see that sample. You may have a beautiful cover and people will oooh and aaah, but the only thing you see is the typo — and you experience only regret about not spending enough time double-checking. Trust me, it hurts badly enough that you only let it happen once. If you hand your creative files to someone who doesn't care about quality, not only will you have to live with their apathy to the final product, but endure the effects on your ego each time you show your work. Make sure the quality of your printer's work reflects favorably on you and your future. You can control this by choosing the right vendor to print your job.

If you did your homework when you first started out, you know who has the right equipment to produce your job. Prior to online services, you were obligated to use a printer in your area. Now digital printers are springing up all over and it's highly competitive. There are high-volume printers all over the country (and the world) waiting to outbid the competition if you give them the chance. The more willing you are to explore the marketplace, the more flexible your scope of services will be for your clients. It's up to you to verify a printer's production standards. But it only takes one poorly executed job to identify the losers.

2. Steer Clear of Print Brokers

Here's a money-saving tip: Stay away from brokers. Print brokers are middlemen who add fees for their services and an extra step between you and the printer. A real advantage freelancers bring to a client roster is lower printing costs. Don't use a print broker instead of doing the footwork yourself. Print brokers earn their fees by knowing who has the best deals in town and using "trade only" print shops.

You are a member of the trade and can access these deals yourself if you know how to properly formulate a set of specs. Get a good book online. You can order the indispensable *Pocket Pal: The Handy Book of Graphic Arts Production* through the website of the International Paper Company, www.ippocketpal.com. Alternatively, sit down with a knowledgeable production manager at a big printing plant. Smart ones will be happy to share their knowledge with potential clients like you. They are also eager to educate you before you bring in work, in case you aren't sure of what you're doing. Again, recent studies suggest that one way printers are recouping lost revenue is through client education and prepress file cleanup. Pay your printer to print the job, not teach you how to do your job.

An accurate set of job specifications is important so that all your bidding vendors are quoting on the same job — you know, the old apples-to-apples comparison. This all falls under the heading of knowing how to produce what you create. You would be surprised how many people don't, especially those who work at big agencies with qualified production managers to do all the work for them. If you haven't left the agency yet, make friends with the production manager. Take this person out to lunch, pick his brain, and find out how you can learn everything he knows about print buying. Production managers are largely responsible for the success or failure of their agency's print profits and can fill you in on all the ins and outs of your local vendors and the print market in general.

3. Watch Out for Tricks of the Trade

There are a few tricks of the trade to watch out for. One common trick in preparing a bid is substituting paper stock at the last minute. Watch for quote forms that discreetly itemize specification formation into "paper stock or similar substitution." Be smart and cross out "similar substitution." If your printer ignores the stock you've specified and quotes the job on something called "a similar coated stock," send the bid back; better yet, ignore the bid and tell the printer why you did.

This is a clear sign that he will disregard your wishes further down the line, and that will get you in trouble with your client. It also shows that the printer is more concerned about his own convenience in job production than he is about meeting a set of specs. Be clear that you represent your client and the client's wishes. Your client is not going to care how the local printer wants to produce a job for his own ease of operation. If you approve the substitution, you may end up explaining to your client why the job doesn't look as promised.

If you spend the time properly selecting stock and getting that selection approved by the client, don't settle for a last-minute substitution to save a few dollars. On the rare chance that there are problems with the stock you selected, consult your local paper representative. You can also go online to a wonderful website that is quickly replacing swatchbooks. Paper Specs Online, www.paper specs.com, founded by Sabine Lenz, offers hundreds of wise tidbits concerning paper selection. There are also specific production notes and a very helpful forum.

On the other hand, if you trust your printer and the issues he raises with the sheet you've selected, talk it over with your paper representative and ask for similar sheets that have comparative costs. It's too tempting for the printer (even one you trust) to suggest you use overages left on the floor from previous jobs.

4. Pay for Quality Printing

You've learned to ignore the printers who say they can print anything, you've learned to recognize a good attitude in a supplier (mainly that you are the customer), and you've learned not to make last-minute substitutions without client consent. But probably the most important thing to learn, aside from having a good working relationship with your suppliers, is that you get what you pay for.

If you want to risk the quality of your job at an instant printer, get ready to explain to your client why the brochures you delivered last week crack at the fold the first time you open one. Picture yourself explaining after the fact that had they just spent that extra hundred dollars, this wouldn't be happening. If they had just let you take the brochure to the slightly higher priced printer you've worked with for years, the brochures would have been printed on paper with the grain going in the right direction. The discerning factor between the two printers was that one put the quality of your job ahead of his need to cut costs. And what about those fingerprints showing up on that high-dollar print piece? Did you stress the importance of a matt varnish to diminish the smudge effect? I have every confidence in you, but remember that whatever goes wrong, no matter how small, will be blamed on you. Knowledge is power, so make sure you have the power to protect yourself.

Low-ball bids are usually formulated through crash scheduling or material cost-cutting. Sometimes the price is slightly lower because the shop buys extremely large quantities of stock and can pass some of the savings on to the customer. On a rare occasion, printers who desperately want to establish a relationship with a client who does a large volume of work will low-ball a bid by doing the job for cost. This is a bona fide method of a printer getting that first job, and it sometimes provides a quality piece at cost for the freelancer. The fallacy is that once the printer has done that initial job, you will never see the same price again, even on a reprint. For the duration of that job, you will be making up the shortfall in cost.

Knowing the motivation for a low-ball price is imperative when accepting a low bid. Scheduling many small jobs together cuts back on make-ready and cleanup costs and allows a small printer to give a blanket reduction across the board. The problem is that not everybody is willing to wait until a print shop has six jobs in the same color ready to run at the same time (gang printing), information he will forget to mention unless asked. The other problem for the freelancer is that printers rarely tell you which of these gimmicks they are using to save money.

Knowledge is power, so make sure you have the power to protect yourself.

Pay particular attention to turnaround times noted on the quote and ask for a revised quote if your client expects the work done sooner. A long turnaround time is a clear indication of gang printing. Many print brokers will offer low-cost promotional postcards with the catch that they take eight weeks to print. The sneaky devils ship the art to Hong Kong and gang print them in a single run on a web press.

A quick comparison of material costs can reveal last-minute substitutions of paper stock or using odd lots of stock left over from previous jobs. Keep your eyes open. Many shops will be tempted to substitute a number two sheet for a number one sheet if they think they can get away with it. (They'll *know* they can get away with it if you submitted a print file in Corel Draw!) Some sheets may have very little visual difference but a drastic difference in ink spread and coverage. Depending on quantities, the shop will be able to pocket hundreds of dollars in profit if they succeed in fooling an unsuspecting client. Most reputable print shops won't even consider such

a move, but if they do, they certainly won't mention it. There are so many behind-the-scenes opportunities for deception, ethics can become very important to your success, so choose someone you can trust. Pay close attention — that's what your client pays you to do. If you don't, there are ten other designers out there who will. Small print shops are particularly bad about using leftovers without mentioning it to a client. It's your responsibility to make sure this doesn't happen, and one way to pre-empt it is by asking the printer to make up a dummy before you give him the job. If the dummy cracks when it's folded, count on it cracking after it's printed. Sometimes such poor quality is just a lack of training, as instant printers rarely can afford to hire qualified help. And sometimes it's just the drive to cut costs in a tough market. No matter what causes it, stand firm, as your client depends on your expertise to maintain standards. Besides, designers have never been known to be overly agreeable as a group. This is the time to pull out your chutzpah.

5. Learn to Talk Like a Printer

Antiquated software isn't printers' only tip-off that they're dealing with an amateur. Learn to speak printer talk. As soon as you make your first phone call, a printer can tell if you know what you're doing by the language you use to describe your job. He will be less likely to try to take advantage of you if you know what you're doing. Let's say you have a four-color job with color to the edge that folds to fit into a standard business envelope. The inside of the brochure has only two colors because you think this will save money, and you are printing a quantity of 10,000 that must be ready in two weeks. How would you describe this over the phone?

Here's the conversation: "Hello, Joe. How are you? Say, I've got this little job, it's an eight and a half by eleven-inch bleed, and I need 10,000 of four over two on 100-pound book Vintage white gloss with a scored letter fold and a 10-day turnaround. Would you work up a quote for me?" You've accurately given your printer all the specifications he needs to correctly formulate a bid, and in language he understands. There will be fewer mistakes and less time invested for everyone involved in the future.

Can you spot the error in planning? There is no cost saving in designing a four over two color brochure on a run this small. Printers do what's called a work and turn, printing both sides of the brochure on a signature sheet. This cuts down on the expense of labor and allows the press to keep running without a plate change or wash-down. They run one side of the paper with both the front and back image, flip the paper, back it up (align the images), then run the same image again. When the paper is trimmed you have a double stack of the same brochure, thus doing twice the work in half the time. This limits your press time expenditure and also makes you look good if you ask, "You'll do a work and turn, right?" Next time, just design the brochure so it's four-color on both sides.

5.1 Use the Jargon of Your Trade

Let's explore the jargon of the design trade, which is rife with killer terms. While I was opening a plastic container the other day to make a quick sandwich, I realized I was having a hard time removing the fugitive glue that held the cardboard identifier to the top of the reusable container. Oh, it wasn't a blister pack, just an insert attached with wads of rubbery glue that temporarily adhered to identify or deliver product packaging. What's with the name — is this because fugitives frequently have sticky fingers, become unglued easily, or because they rarely stick around for long? The thought of this wacky nomenclature drew me into the wide assortment of brutal terms used in our industry.

Someone brought up the violator, which used to be called a burst. Bursts were supposed to make you think the product improvement was so recent, they had to apply a sticker to the box just coming off the conveyor. I suppose some designer was so put off by the addition of a tired old starburst in their design that they might have felt violated. I suppose having a graphic violator imposed on your design might make you want to just die, as in the male and female die used in embossing. This brings to mind some maniac standing on top of a victim, shouting, "Die, die, die!" as he stabs them to death, or should that be clobbers them to death using a slug? Would the murderer be required to jump on a deadline and nail it? Did the victim leave a widow? Nah, the dummy was a dropout. His name was Doctor Blade.

Over at the print shop, they speak like killers and brutes, too, using terms like trapping, shooting stick, dead-on, knockout, hanging (up or in), hits, frayed, scuffed, hits, slur or burn; and when that's all done, they put your stock on the guillotine for a nice trim, just like they gave Marie Antoinette. But no worries, they always break for color.

Photography, too, toys with gory words like head shot, blow-up, and shoot — at least they do it at a distance and don't get their hands bloody. We've got the bleed, punch, strike, stretcher, sniping, and dead color. Oh, that's messy. Have we hit the skids or been reamed? Take that, I'm going to whack you with a stack of 500 sheets of paper!

My favorite phrases describe any component of the process that conspires against reason to put ink on the nonprinting part of a plate, and then transfer unwanted scum onto the sheet. Scum is a greasy film that sensitizes non-image areas into accepting ink when it's got no business doing so — an irritating nuisance.

If I use laid paper for a reproduction proof, will it prevent issuance and reproduction? And another thing, did you get all those hickeys rolling around in the gutter? If you can't figure out what these graphic terms mean, spend some time with International Paper's *Pocket Pal* or Google the terms you don't understand. They are all pertinent to the trade.

6. Get the Best Deal for Your Client

Sometimes, the printer you want to work with doesn't submit a competitive quote. This usually happens when you've been using the same printer for a long time and he grows complacent with the account. He's no longer interested in cost savings for the client; he's only interested in doing a good job and making a profit. Keeping you happy with a rock-bottom price is no longer of prime importance. Don't be hard on him, though, because sometimes he's just concentrating on doing the job the best way possible.

Don't forget you serve the client's interests while you're being wined and dined by your print shop. It's your responsibility to negotiate the best possible deal. After you've solicited bids, an opportunity always exists for negotiation. Review the bids carefully, weeding out any substitutions and quotes that are unusually high or low. Bids that are way off are usually the result of a calculation error or misunderstood specification. Be fair and call the printer back. Point out the comparative aberration so they can correct it if they want to remain in the running. It is completely proper for you to call the printer you want to work with at this point and tell him he isn't getting the job because his price is too high. If he really wants the work, or suspects there's been a miscalculation, he will most likely check his figures and submit another bid. Printers want your work, and if you tell them where they're at in the running, they will gladly resubmit a reworked, double-checked price. Your efforts will profit your client and your client relationship because you've just delivered quality and savings.

7. Collect Your Sales Commission

There's one more thing you'll need to learn about negotiating with your suppliers. Some people call it a sales commission and others call it a carrying charge. Unfortunately, some call it a kickback or payoff, too. Either way, ad agencies and design studios mark up all subcontractor work by 15 to 45 percent, depending on the market. Recently, a lot has been written about the ethics surrounding this practice. It has been a trade practice since the invention of the printing press. Your local department store marks up clothing by 75 percent, and they have no qualms about taking your money.

As a freelancer, you have to negotiate with the printer, make stock selections, monitor separation quality, do press checks, and coordinate delivery times, all the while calming and reassuring your client — all off the clock. It's off the clock because it's nearly impossible to keep track of the time spent nursing a job that's in production, tweaking the details so it all comes to fruition. Your expertise guarantees the quality of the product you provide, and a 15 percent markup is proper compensation for this. If you have moral issues with markups, then tell your client that you require a 15 percent commission to cover extra time spent with prepress production details, the printer, and press checks. Either way, you should be paid for services rendered. (Calculating and collecting markups is covered in more depth in Chapter 10.)

After all, if your client handled his own printing, he wouldn't know if his job was printed on a sheet with the grain going the right way or a sheet the printer had left over from his last job. Your accumulated experience helps prevent the unexpected. Subcontractor fees are marked up across the board, and unless you took a vow of poverty when you decided to freelance, you should collect your just due.

NINE SURE SIGNS YOU'RE NOT GETTING PAID

There are many signs to look for when things have gone sour in a creative working relationship. I don't cover obvious signs in this chapter, like an invoice that's gone past due for more than 120 days or the fact that your client's office was emptied by a moving van the day after the job was delivered. When people resort to avoidance tactics, the game's over and you don't need my advice to see you won't be getting paid. Likewise when your client won't take your calls, it's a sure bet you won't be paid.

The nine signs you aren't going to be paid that I describe are more subtle — little things your gut picks up on but your sentimentality convinces you to ignore. Don't be a party to denying your instincts. Learn to trust yourself. Memorize these signs and train yourself to go into a cold sweat when you see one. When you sense something is wrong, decide how you want to handle it. Ask yourself the following questions:

- How will you confront your client without alienating him or her just in case you're wrong?

- Is it worth the trouble or should you let things ride?

- Do you like your client enough to let it go if he or she doesn't pay?

It is almost never worth the trouble of suing someone you've worked with for years and who has suddenly fallen on hard times.

Sometimes it's worth it to get a handle on your feelings about these issues before you decide on a plan of action. Unless you're from the planet Vulcan and your name is Spock, in which case your emotions are completely in check, never broach the subject until you have formulated a plan of action.

From personal experience, I can tell you it's almost never worth the trouble of suing someone you've worked with for years and who has suddenly fallen on hard times. Be generous of spirit enough to realize that over the years, you've made enough money on that client to ignore a default on a couple of jobs. You'll recognize time-tested dead giveaways in the stories that follow. Learn from them and recognize the signs and signals that hope for cash should be dashed. History has shown that no matter how experienced or adept you are at reading human behavior, these nine signs will sneak up and bite you before you know it.

1. Delay — "The Check Is in the Mail"

Even when you do a fair day's work, there are people out there who revel in getting something for nothing. They can't be avoided. Their only goal is to get a deal (either by wheeling and dealing or just plain stealing) or get something for nothing. It's surprising the number of people who pride themselves on delaying payment for as long as they can. Talk to anyone who works for the gas company, and they will tell you some of the richest people are the hardest to collect from. Human behavior can be skewed when it comes to money, so expect the worst when collecting from individuals.

By and large, companies have professional staff who handle invoices, and unless the middle manager is sadly disappointed with the service you rendered, your invoice has been approved and sent to accounts payable for payment processing. But a professional accounting staff does not by any means guarantee payment. Delay of any kind can be a dead giveaway that trouble lurks behind the scenes.

The work I did for one big-city architectural firm that designed a large part of downtown Houston suddenly started slow-paying invoices that used to be paid like clockwork at 30 days. Now they were dragging on to 45 and 60 days. One job in particular was a spiral-bound calendar on heavy stock, each month heralded with a line illustration of one of the firm's projects. At 60 days, I took a walk with one of the junior interior designers and he confessed the firm was seconds away from declaring bankruptcy. He went with me to the accounting department and my invoice was paid immediately, but I had to offer them a 10 percent discount to motivate them.

1.1 Act fast in the case of bankruptcy

When the word "bankruptcy" comes up, speed is of the essence. Creditors have to file a claim and are paid in order of importance. The government is always first, the lawyers and trustee are second, and any secured debt is third. Creative services are unsecured debt, so plan on getting into a long line. If you are number 257 on the list of unsecured creditors, you'll be lucky if you get anything except the costly opportunity to file a claim. So don't wait before you pick up the phone and speak to the person you worked with on the project.

Sometimes the right person will have some pull with the powers in charge and can force a payout. Be willing to give a small discount for quick payment. After picking up the check, take it immediately to the bank it was drawn on and cash it. Hopefully your relationship with the client is good enough to warrant extraordinary efforts on your behalf. Keep in mind, any payments received within 90 days of a bankruptcy filing are subject to review by the trustee assigned to the case. This usually happens only if there was a large, noticeable outlay of capital paid to a single creditor. Ordinary operation expenses rarely attract attention.

If you suspect bankruptcy but have no confirmation, here's a tip: A sudden rush to project completion and doubling of quantities on standard orders is usually to ensure sufficient stock to continue business long past the time a trustee freezes a company's bank accounts. Do a credit check or quietly ask around for signs of trouble, like disconnected phones, sudden layoffs of long-term employees, or downsizing office space. If the person you usually work with suddenly takes a job with a competing firm, this can also be a sign of trouble. Be alert to the signs.

1.2 Late payment can be intentional

Frequently, delay is by design. I did two small jobs for a string of big-city physical rehabilitation clinics. I made sure they had all the right forms and were billed in triplicate and waited for the check to roll in. After 45 days, I called the company. I got an automated system where I could key in my invoice amount and find out where it was in the system. Guess what? It wasn't in the system. I called back and spoke with the manager of accounts payable, who told me she couldn't process my invoice until I had a vendor number. To get a vendor number, I had to fill in a form, mail it, and wait until they had time to enter it.

Another month went by and no check. I called and asked for my vendor number, keyed it into the system, and still the two-month-old invoice was not in the system. I spoke with the same manager again and was told they had my invoice, but it had not been approved by the local manager. When I called the local manager, he reassured me he had approved my invoice the day he received it and that he would call the accounts payable manager immediately to correct the situation. She faxed him a copy; he signed it and faxed it back. I waited for the check to show up, and after another 15 days, I called the accounts payable manager. When I reminded her of the faxed approval, the vendor number delay, and how long past due the invoices were, she stopped midway through her next excuse and said she would have to look into why the invoice had not been paid.

When the check came, it was for only one invoice, so I had to start the whole process over again. I eventually got my payment, but the small printer and typesetter who billed direct gave up and wrote it off. This is when you have to listen to your instincts and trust your gut reaction that the delays are intentional. Businesses that are slow payers are generally bad customers. The old adage that if the office personnel are rude, the doctor probably is, too, is true.

This much delay in paying an invoice is by design, not accident, and is dictated by senior management to restrict cash outlay to a minimum. Unless you have the fortitude of a Russian shotputter, avoid companies like this no matter how nice the assignment. If you don't, you'll end up spending more time in accounting functions than you do creatively — and that's annoying. If you want to keep this client in spite of the repeated delay, do what a nearly famous 3-D illustrator does: "After repeated instances of late payment, I systematically add an agony factor to each invoice, sometimes as much as 30 percent to cover all that time I know I will have to spend trying to collect. That hurts them even more because I always give clients a 3 percent discount for early payment. It would be easier if they would just take advantage of that."

Most companies pay their bills on time, and counting a few big ones among your clients quiets any insecurity you may have regarding where your next job is coming from. When billing a big company, it's always best to send the invoice to the person you did the work for; that way they know the bill accurately reflects what the two of you agreed on prior to commencing the work. If they enjoy the service and quality you gave them, they will be sure to expedite your invoice.

1.3 Protect yourself with a retainer

The "unaffiliated individual" is a potential bad risk, and if you accept work on trust, you can count on negotiating for a percentage of leftovers if the business fails. There are certain things you can do to make sure you don't walk away empty-handed when accepting work from a start-up or entrepreneur. The first and most obvious: only work on a retainer basis. One freelance writer I know has an ironclad contract that even spells out the number of revisions and the minimum amount of retainer she will accept for each project. She won't even discuss the project until all the paperwork is signed.

A retainer puts the cash in hand before you spend any of your nonrefundable time on the client's project.

A contract sounds like a good idea until you realize it's still just a piece of paper. If your client defaults, you may have to hire a lawyer to enforce the contract. A retainer puts the cash in hand before you spend any of your nonrefundable time on the client's project. How much of a retainer do you want? If it's an individual, ask for at least half of the total project cost in advance before any work is started. Don't be surprised if they balk. That's a quick give-away that they weren't committed to the project anyway and they certainly aren't committed to paying you for your time. In fact, it may be a sign that they can't afford the expenditure at all; you may have exposed a con or something more innocent — the wishful thinker. Be grateful for your own insight and run as fast as you can.

Another helpful backup in the quest for payment is a time sheet. Keep a time sheet for each project and review it with your client as the retainer is used up. Don't make the mistake of continuing to work on a project when the retainer in your bank account has not been refreshed. Remember at all times that you are doing this for a living and that love doesn't pay the bills. Quick to compliment but slow to pay means only one thing — there's a snake in the grass.

A few more words about contracts: Many books and organizations advocate the use of these wonderful legal documents because they spell out the responsibilities of both parties, their limitations, and their expectations. The problem is that a contract does two things just by its introduction. First, it alienates both parties. By

You can only enforce a contract by going to court. Is it worth the time and expense?

admitting the need for a contract, you've already established a lack of trust. Second, it automatically obligates you to buy legal services. No matter what happens to cause you to fall back on the contract to collect, you must pay a lawyer to execute the contract, pay court fees, pay filing fees, and so on. If you want to spend your time interfacing with lawyers and courtrooms, use a contract. If you want to do design work and guarantee you'll be paid for it, ask for a retainer up front.

2. The Ties That Bind

How hard can it be to get paid? Some creative professionals will tell you that's the hardest part of their jobs, while others say they have never had a problem. One thing for sure, family and friends really don't want to pay you. Even the remotest friend, perhaps someone you would call a passing acquaintance, will expect you to discount the cost of your services. After all, it's a God-given talent, isn't it? Just think if the electric company would supply the power you need because you have this talent. Either expect to do the job for free and be pleasantly surprised if you get paid or just refer them to someone else. The best way to work around this expectation when you don't want to donate your services is to beg off by saying you are far too expensive for them and laugh yourself out of the room. Then congratulate yourself on avoiding a close call.

3. The Ignored Invoice

Some work won't pay off regardless of how good your relationship is with your client. My job at a big company ended and I put the word out I was looking for freelance assignments. This wasn't my first stint as a freelancer, and I was clearly familiar with the ropes. I got a call from one of the big bosses at the company I used to work for. He wanted to help his brother start a business and asked me to throw my best efforts into his corporate identity and promotional materials. "Now, I expect you to do your best work, as you will be partly responsible for the success or failure of the project," he said.

Nobody is more susceptible to managerial motivation than creatives, so I threw my heart and soul into developing a corporate identity for his brother's business. I offered my client a deal of a flat rate to design the logo, letterhead, business envelope, and business card, provided he sent me a retainer. He said fine. Two weeks went by and no check arrived, but the work progressed and I was in daily contact with his brother, reviewing designs and answering questions, giving him advice on various projects not covered by the retainer, and soliciting prices from vendors. So I dropped my client a line and mentioned the retainer. He said he didn't object, but he wanted an invoice from me with a record of the retainer and when it was used up. I agreed. Again, how this delay is a dead giveaway will become apparent. Note here that people in financial circles are experts at setting up overlapping delays to create questionable collection circumstances — so be wary. Five days later, and after the start of several Yellow Pages ads and some truck signage that wasn't included in the flat fee arrangement, the check arrived. By this time, his brother had not only used up the retainer, but spent another $1,500 on pricing presentation folders, T-shirts, caps, designing signage, proposal paper, memo pads, photo retouching, etc., I carefully printed out a list of files and their creation dates, listed the work done, subtracted the retainer, and put the invoice in a priority package that I speedily shipped to my client.

A few days later, his brother casually asked if the retainer was used up. I knew this meant trouble. "I sent an invoice last week. Not only is the retainer used up, there's a balance due and owing. Didn't you get a ten-pound box of homemade cookies?" Well, yes, they had received the cookies, but his brother hadn't mention anything about an invoice.

Always pay attention, because the human mind wants to believe in the good of humanity. When someone gives you clues about what's coming, believe it, don't deny it to yourself. I ignored it when my client said he would send the retainer and didn't; then I ignored it when he received an invoice he didn't notice, and didn't respond to. There's another lesson hidden in all this action. Can you see it? My client negotiated a flat fee for corporate development and loaded me up with additional projects not included in that fee. Whether this was intentional or just the push to get things done, the end result was the same. I did a lot of work I didn't get paid for. There was only one stupid person in that scenario, and I hope you can learn from my mistakes.

4. Rush to Project Completion

When my client claimed to have "missed" the invoice, I resent it in good faith. (My perpetual belief that people are good must stem from my Catholic upbringing, but it's better to be a pessimist in business.) I expected to receive a check, since my client's brother was now piling on the work. There is no point in a client relationship when it is okay to foot-drag, especially when most things are done on deadline. But you have to get a grip on yourself and just stop working when they stop paying. All of a sudden, in spite of unresolved billing issues, my client had a schedule. It was Wednesday when he suddenly needed his brochure by Friday to stick to his schedule.

Schedule? This was his first mention of a schedule in two months of work. I knew it was a ploy, but you know how it is when you enjoy what you're doing. I trusted my friend, trusted my friend's brother, and trusted they would take care of me by paying their bill with as much diligence as I was showing in taking care of them. Looking back, I'm sure this guy knew this, maybe even counted on my sense of responsibility to deadlines. A week later when the check finally came, it was for much less than the amount owed. I stopped working on the project, sent them a backup disk for the file I had completed, and wished them good luck. Keep in mind that even when your client defaults on payment, it's best to maintain your professionalism right up to and including delivery of the files on disk.

5. Triangulation

Freelancers have to protect themselves from what I call peripheral involvements. Whether the younger brother was taking advantage of me, knowing his brother wasn't going to pay, or whether the older brother privately scolded his younger brother for giving me more work than he wanted to pay for, I was left holding the bag — and it was empty.

Never let another person act as liaison between you and your client. Sometimes it's impossible to change an arrangement, but you can copy that person on all correspondence, keep track of meetings, and forward all project information, changes, and cost updates. Find a way to get around the third party so everybody is on the same page. There's no sure way to prevent triangulation other than to avoid the situation altogether. Make sure all parties are privy to decisions regarding project scope, payment, and completion, no matter how much they complain about the excessive amount of correspondence.

Here's another example of triangulation: A friend called me excited because her sister, married to a big Florida developer, needed a logo designed for some beachside property. I was excited, too, because I usually got to design medical product logos, and this was fresh and exciting. So I started working up logos and sent the first weeks' spectrum of possibilities to her sister by priority mail. (Locking down the direction your client wants to go with a logo, then refining it with each redesign, prevents what many designers call "the endless search for what your client has in mind but cannot communicate.") I gave both parties a set of printouts so they could talk about things on the phone. They were pleased with my logos and talked about them enthusiastically.

About a week later, curious that I hadn't heard from my friend, I asked if they were ready to select from the samples and be presented with a second series. "Oh, I'm sorry. I've been putting off calling you with some bad news. My sister's husband contracted with another designer a week earlier and she can't use your designs because he's already obligated." I was told to send my bill. Instead of billing my usual flat rate for logo design, I decided to be reasonable under the circumstances and bill for half the hours spent, thus saving them 50 percent of the fee and hopefully encouraging them to get this issue behind us quickly so we could all move on in the friendship. I've found that when a project is cancelled due to an innocent misunderstanding, goodwill in reducing the invoice usually lubricates the pen of the paying party.

If the worst happens and the bill goes unpaid, it's best to forget about it.

In this case, my friend turned out to be a classic rube. I got a check about a month later with a note telling me she was paying less than half of her already halved invoice because she didn't want to upset her husband. And she was using her own money — indicating she was used to spending other people's. I had no recourse in this situation, having never spoken to the contracting party. I had been triangulated by a friend and suffered the consequences of violating two of the sure signs.

If the worst happens and the bill goes unpaid, it's best to forget about it instead of stewing over it. If you've been caught in this kind of a triangle, there's no hope of proving an understanding existed or that the assignment was ever agreed to by the original party. Cut your losses and don't invest any more time in it.

It is not the responsibility of creative professionals to reduce their fees after the work is done.

6. Reasoning Plus Excuses

The client who wanted me to download his competition's photography for his brochure suggested an after-the-fact work-around. He said he would poll creatives in his area to see how much it would cost to have the work done locally. This is the first step in rationalizing nonpayment when the client doesn't want to pay the bill, especially when the price has been agreed to in advance.

The next act in this scenario is ugly. To justify his behavior, the client starts to criticize the work. It can get gruesome, but if you always deliver your best work, you know in your heart his gibes are false. This only happens after you've quoted your rates in advance and have already completed most of the project. The exercise serves only to bolster the client's ego after he's opted out of doing the right thing. Remember, there are people in every industry who will do the job for less.

It's up to the client to decide before the work is done who gets the assignment. If he only wants to pay $50 per hour, he should hire a creative who charges that rate. It is not the responsibility of creative professionals to reduce their fees after the work is done. It's a bad idea to cast pearls before swine anyway, so don't reduce your rates to meet unreasonable expectations.

Again, if you want to spend your time chasing after a few dollars, take the client to court. It will be a challenge to show evidence that an agreement was ever reached initially, since so much work was probably added above and beyond what was included in the original quote. Then you have to deal with clients who are moving facts to suit their objective. Try to develop an instinct for spotting cheapskates, but count on meeting a few bottom dwellers like the ones I've described here.

7. The Bold-Faced Lie

"Yes, I received your invoice and the check is in the mail." How many times have you heard that? The job is complete, you didn't get a retainer, the product has been delivered, and your client never had any intention of paying for it. There's no way to predict this behavior other than gut reaction, but be forewarned and listen to your instincts. If you pick up the slightest queasy feeling, get that retainer up front — and preferably in cash — or decline the job.

If you think this won't happen to you, guess again. The sad thing is, you'll never see it coming. I designed a press kit and assorted pieces for a luxury airliner. I did the work for an acquaintance (second sign, shame on me) whom I had worked with who had rich relatives. They wanted the best of everything. Everything they ordered had gold foil stamping, blind embossing, and custom cuts. They used a number one text sheet and Crane's 100 percent rag paper. I called my friend and he said it — in the mail, yessiree. Within two months, the planes were empty and none of the invoices were paid. I called my friend and found the offices empty except for the chief financial officer.

Warning, Will Robinson: Know in advance that it is a CFO's responsibility to bargain down the price of debts when the rats are jumping ship. He was ever so polite as he said he could cut me a check that day if I was willing to give him a discount. I gave him a 20 percent discount and I got my check, but the printer had to go as low as 50 percent, losing all his labor costs, to collect enough to pay for the paper. Most CFOs will jump at any discount, so start very low and work up as his motivation grows. Just be sure you're one of the first people to call, because when the money is gone, it's gone for good. If you sense things are deteriorating fast (and speaking to the CFO about a past due invoice is a sure sign), offer to pick up the check in person later that day.

8. Price Is No Object

Unless your client's last name is DuPont or Rockefeller, or you have copies of the client's last four platinum CDs, price is always a consideration no matter what the client tells you. Of the three lawsuits I filed before I realized that only my lawyer was making money, two of the clients started their projects by saying money was no object. In fact, they stressed they wanted the best of everything. Another way the abundant attitude of "give me all you've got" rears its ugly head is by scoffing at your repeated mention of the amount of money spent at various points during project development. "Oh, don't worry about that. I'm not worried about it!" (I have found this usually means they aren't worried because they have no intention of paying anyway!)

Frequent reviews of time sheets and accumulated hours are a necessary and normal part of your client relationship. They're also your responsibility if you want to get paid. Clients with big ideas and empty purses can't resist pushing the envelope. It's just an extension of the more general problem of living beyond their means. Do not fall prey to donating your time to a dreamer in denial. If worse comes to worst, believe they'll pay for the Rolls before they pay you.

9. The Empty Promise of Future Work

Old pros laugh about this one as it never seems to go away, and people say it with such sincerity. You've jumped through flaming hoops for your client and he hasn't paid his bill. When you call at 60 days, he tells you: "You're next to be paid and don't worry, I love your work and don't want to do anything to upset you. I can't wait to go over that big brochure we'll be starting next week."

Warning: If you have just completed a project that you haven't been paid for, get a grip on your excitement about another project you might not get and certainly won't get paid for. You are being manipulated into providing free labor. Learn to react to the promise of upcoming work with polite trepidation when it comes from a debtor. A client may say, "Yes, I know you haven't been paid yet, but you'll get that next big job that's coming up later this month." For the phrase "that next big job," substitute the words "more unpaid work" in your own mind. Or add "Free labor, moron" at the end of the sentence, because you're ignoring your gut instinct that this is a delaying mechanism and nothing more. Pretend the idle promises have those phrases attached, and that feeling of excitement will fade. A new sense of reality will descend and you will return your focus to paying clients with real work.

9.1 Be up front about payment details

Speak to your clients about your expectations at the beginning of the job. As much as you want to make their expectations the focus of your service, you must ensure a clear understanding of billing practices and procedures. As much as we all would like to conduct business on trust and a handshake, it's just not sound business practice in today's turbulent economy. Nobody likes to talk about money, but creativity is a business just like any other, and it's important to spell out the rules of the game.

9.2 Keep your client well informed

Make sure you keep records of the time spent, inform your client as soon as a retainer is spent, and apprise your client of the progress of the job and any problems you foresee before the assignment is complete. A good client will understand and do the right thing if you take the time to update him while a project is ongoing. It's okay to lose a bad client and it's mandatory to get rid of a nonpaying client. Getting a client to sign a contract is a nice idea if you have money to hire the lawyer to go to court when the contract is breached; you *may* collect a couple of years after the fact if there's anything left after you paid counsel. But a better idea is to pay attention to warning signs and avoid the dilemma altogether.

Chapter 10

FEES AND WHAT TO DO WHEN THE CLIENT DOESN'T DO THE RIGHT THING

When you work freelance, for the first time in your life you will decide what your services are worth and what you want to earn. Don't price yourself out of the market, but don't charge the same rate as someone with half your education and a tenth of your creative depth. One practical method is to sit down and decide how many hours you want to work each week, then compute what you expect to have in your bank account at the end of the month.

Remember when you are working out a standard fee schedule to include any state or provincial and local taxes, federal income taxes, and social security. Sometimes it's easier to look at these numbers as a retailer would. Follow these steps:

1. Determine how much money you want for your work. (Don't forget to include the built-in equity.)

2. Add on extraneous money you have to collect for third parties such as the government.

Some states require sales tax on professional services, so investigate what's required in your area. (In Canada, depending on your income, you may need to apply for a goods and services tax [GST] number.) A good tax accountant who specializes in creative services will help you figure all this out. Trust a professional, as the tax laws change every year and you may be paying more than you should if

One certainty in freelancing is your firm right to decide how much you want to be paid.

you do your own return. Almost everything you buy that can be construed as relating to your work is tax deductible.

The two basic rules of business apply to self-employment and freelancing if you're trying to make a living. Follow them, and success is within easy reach. In the words of professional photographer Dennis Meyler: "The first [rule] is have something someone wants to buy. The second is your income must exceed your outgo." Meyler grew his business over the years by extending his skills to three-dimensional illustration. To balance the flow of money collected and money spent, don't spend money that's "in the mail" until you have it firmly in hand.

Do the necessary soul-searching and determine your unique product, evaluate your skills, and assess your strengths and weaknesses. Once you complete this personal inventory, you'll better be able to decide how you compare with the competition and how to make sure your fees are fair and equitable. Don't rely on books to set your price — information contained in books and magazine articles is subjective and based on limited polls taken in specific metropolitan areas. Also, the information quickly becomes dated. Instead, find out what the successful competition charges and then weigh their education and experience against your own. You may decide to charge more or less, depending on how you stack up against the competition. If you bring 20-odd years of agency experience to the table plus a solid college education, you should be charging as much as an established lawyer, depending on your skill set. Never forget that one certainty in freelancing is your firm right to decide how much you want to be paid. It doesn't matter if Joe Blow down the street will do it for less; your product and expertise are unique and should be determined independently. If you aren't making enough money, raise your rates. This may be the first time your destiny (and your pocketbook) are firmly in your own control.

1. Dealing with Subcontractors and Clients

If you've ever parted with a client, you know the feeling of loss for all the things you did above and beyond invoiced hours to cement the relationship. You did this so goodwill might maintain the relationship. There are good clients and bad clients, and if it's a mystery to you why a client walked, then it probably didn't have anything to do with you or your work. People don't always pick their creative help because of talent. Politics, personal prejudice, nepotism, and stupidity are equal motivators in human behavior. Client behavior can be silly and arbitrary, but since you devote time to finding new business each week, losing a client won't threaten your peace of mind or your livelihood.

After you lose your first client to a peer, you'll learn to appreciate the cardinal rule of the freelance world: the person who finds the job *claims the client*. Just as in life, ethical common sense is *uncommon*. For example, a writer or illustrator who worked closely with *your client* on the last brochure may walk away with the next project because he thinks of himself as a free agent. He hasn't learned that his peers will no longer throw work his way if, by doing so, they risk losing a client. I guarantee you will feel pretty helpless when you find out a client you haven't heard from in a long time is using the web developer's sexy girlfriend for services you once provided. Short of working with only a few trustworthy people, there *is* a practical work-around to keep this from happening again.

There's no way to prevent a subcontractor from assuming control of a client who has no loyalty to you, is easily swayed, or chooses creative services by price alone. Plenty of people in the world have no scruples or will go to any length to get a better deal. You can lessen the chance of losing a client in this way by locking in your subcontractor's loyalty.

1.1 Dealing with abusive or demanding clients

Have you ever had to deal with abusive or demanding clients? You know the ones I mean; they call at all hours of the night, they show up unannounced, and they see you not as their creative servicer but as a life crutch. Then there are those who constantly show up late for meetings, stay long after the meeting is over, make unreasonable demands, and then blame you for not meeting their expectations. You will occasionally net the client who has no idea what the term "parameters of service" means. When that happens, it's up to you to become parent and teacher. Instead of letting them dominate your life, stop taking the after-hours calls; in fact, wait a day to return those calls if they've gotten out of hand.

When clients show up at your door unannounced, be polite, but don't accommodate them unless it's convenient; ask them to call in advance and make an appointment, then shut the door. It's up to you to make the rules and ask them to respect your wishes — an appointment is mandatory. It is of prime importance to be self-determining and set up boundaries to prevent the bad client from interfering with the work you do for other good clients. This includes the bad client who drags his or her feet when paying your invoice or complains incessantly about the cost of your services. Send that one away. Let's face it, clients are human beings and everybody, even a good client, is capable of going overboard with enthusiasm for a project or with their behavior in general. Their excitement is good, but when it becomes an all-consuming habit, it's up to you to apply the brakes.

Remember, too, that not everybody is willing to abide by your requests and such occasions may require client divorce. Divorce is a good word for it because I don't know anyone who doesn't feel like they've just broken up with a significant other when client ties are cut. The nature of this type of work requires close communication and this intimacy in a successful relationship is hard to abandon. But never let demanding clients ruin your enthusiasm for your work; close them out of your circle by introducing them to somebody else's circle. Give them a short list of alternative designers and give the alternative players a quick call to warn them to set limits at the outset in no uncertain terms. If you do this successfully, the bad clients who learn their lesson will return on their best behavior just to avoid having to start anew. It doesn't pay to be rude or abusive or burn your bridges. But it does pay in the long run to remove the disrespect and boundary bashing from your life experience, so do what you must to maintain homeostasis.

1.2 Your client's bills: To carry or not to carry

One way to shift the loyalty fulcrum point from the client to you is to carry your client's bills. That means all subcontractors bill you instead of billing your client directly. Subcontractors now answer to you and look to you for payment; it becomes crystal clear that you are the client, not to mention the source of other potential projects in the future. Your subcontractor now represents you each time he or she interfaces with your client. Some agencies take this as far as printing up business cards for the contractor. But as long as you're working with people you trust and who understand the potential risks and losses of this relationship, these types of liaisons can work well for all parties.

There are risks involved with carrying another business's invoices, just as there are rewards. The rewards arrive every month when you take a percentage of the total billing in addition to the charges for any creative services rendered. Most agencies and studios are so focused on pushing this benefit to the maximum, they calculate their percentage so they profit not from the net, but from the gross. Agency markups can range from 15 percent to 45 percent depending on agency policy. As a freelancer, set your own policy just as you set your hourly fee. For instance, let's say the Im-a-genius Ad Agency marks up its subcontractors' work by 15 percent. The formula for correctly calculating the profit is the copywriting fee plus the printing bill times 0.1765. This will give you 15 percent of the gross. If your client spent $2,000 on copywriting and $25,000 on printing, add those two figures and multiply by 0.1765 to find the amount of your agency markup to add to the customer invoice. The price you quote to your client is $31,765.50. Your profit on handling these jobs is $4,765.50.

As a freelancing creative, you have the power to determine your own policy and procedures.

Much has been written about markups and sales commissions, sometimes demonizing the practice, but you have to decide for yourself. Will your client look favorably on paying you for every hour you spend following your job from writer's carriage to printer's dock? Probably not. In fact, it's challenging to keep track of the time investment. How will you be compensated on a sliding scale for your years of expertise and the errors your experience prevents, not to mention the quality it ensures? There is no better way than adding a percentage of the cost of printing and subcontractors' labor.

Markups have also been nefariously characterized as kickbacks and payoffs, but they are a legitimate trade practice and sometimes mean the difference between an operation that makes a profit and one that goes into the red. Few agencies handle print jobs without adding the agency commission. Few note the markup on their service invoices, and when they do, it's to avoid even the appearance of impropriety. You may ask yourself why successful agencies that have no problem with their markups don't take a stand and support the practice. As experts, they know attracting attention to a prolific industry-wide practice that adds 15 percent to 45 percent to their clients' bills might work against them, so why risk drawing attention to it? Everybody does it, but standing up and admitting publicly that *you* do it, too, might cause misunderstandings and make some of your clients feel like they've been scalped.

Decide whether you will carry your clients' bills for the control it gives you over subcontractors and the extra profit you realize or whether you will leave that money on the table. If you think this is a moral issue, suggest to your printer that he or she forgo the usual markups on outside services purchased for your jobs, such as

bindery services, foil stamping, or embossing. The printer will probably laugh you right out of the room. Remember the old adage, "No risk, no gain," because it truly applies here. As a freelancing creative, you have the power to determine your own policy and procedures.

1.3 Let the printer carry the risk

You can avoid some of the risk of carrying other people's bills if you have an excellent relationship with a printer you can trust. He or she may be willing to collect your percentage for you. As your jobs move toward the high dollar, your printer may encourage the practice so he or she is in control of the cash (and carrying his or her own risk). This makes good sense, because there is a great cost outlay in paper stock and labor charges. Printers call this percentage your sales commission, but I have waited as long as a year to be reimbursed. The only certainty is that some folks play power games with money, and even those with the best of intentions will use your commission to pay their electricity bill when they have cash flow problems.

2. How to Handle Nonpayment of an Invoice

Now that you see the gain in taking a commission, be forewarned about the risk. Sometimes a client reneges on an invoice and you will be responsible for making good with your suppliers. This is when having a good relationship with your suppliers really makes a difference in your quality of life. During one sudden downturn in the economy, I was heavily involved with oil and gas clients who were going out of business in droves. I was left unpaid and owing. Every economic downturn weeds out the financially weak and monetarily overextended, and many small businesses go under. You can either jump up and down, throw little tantrums, and make a real pest out of yourself with demands for payment that nobody can meet, or you can be patient and polite.

2.1 Exercise empathy, especially in a bad economy

It helps to have a broad perspective and understand economic realities. People can get nasty when you owe them money, and nastiness makes it less likely they will be paid and more likely they will be skipped over for jobs in the future. I learned the hard way that everyone *always* wants to do the right thing, but sometimes it just isn't possible. If businesses are failing, understand that the situation

> If a business fails and can't pay your bill, the best policy is to concentrate on finding other profitable opportunities as quickly as possible.

is bigger than you or what you can change. In particular, remember that after your first angry collection call.

One nearly famous designer offered to do a job for a big charity pro bono, asking only that they pay their typesetting bill. After the type bill went owing for more than 60 days and the charity was still unable to pay, he made an appearance on a big-city news show's "Consumer Watch" segment. He came off as person who was willing to embarrass both himself and his clients in an effort to collect a past due invoice. He lost most of his clients and became an industry embarrassment.

What if you couldn't pay your bill? Would you risk working with this designer knowing how he handles difficult situations? Besides, a recent US test case set a precedent for this situation. Once you air somebody's dirty laundry about money owed, the debt becomes part of the public domain. It is no longer collectible unless you can collect from the public at large.

Whatever the reason people don't pay — a sluggish economy, bad management, or plain stupidity — try to put yourself in their shoes. How would you like to be treated if circumstances beyond your control made it impossible for you to pay your bills? Whether you owe or are owed, if you become abusive and punishing in an effort to collect, both parties lose. Vengeful and vindictive behavior is only suitable on soap operas. In business, as in life, the best policy is to concentrate on finding other profitable opportunities as quickly as possible.

The oil industry is particularly susceptible to economic down-swings. In the early '80s, companies I did business with for years started closing their doors. Wildcat oilmen who had made their fortunes and lived extravagantly were suddenly searching for their next car payment. Once sought after and highly paid, some engineers were living in their cars on the streets of downtown Houston. Commercial real estate values plummeted overnight as tenants decamped, leaving many of the city's skyscrapers vacant. There is no way to predict when the economy will go sour or the country will go to war, but history has proven both events bring commerce to a standstill in the age of CNN. The best policy is to scramble for new business wherever you can and keep your cash inflow above your cash outflow. Keep in mind that nobody wants to leave an unpaid bill, but if you beat them with a big stick over it, chances are they will feel justified in *not* paying you because they've already paid with the grief and contrition you caused trying to collect. Alienation

is the biggest cause of debt apathy. Emote a little empathy or you may be rewarded with abundant apathy.

There is a better way. Keep in mind that creditors consider you just as much a cretin for $125 as for $125,000, so don't default unless you default big. Otherwise, try to work out a payment plan with suppliers. Most suppliers are smart enough to realize that you might be a good client again when things turn around. Design firm frequently trade design work for outstanding printing bills. One well-known studio worked a deal with a printer who owed them some large commissions that produced a 50-page perfect-bound promo piece in quantities large enough to blanket the State of Texas. Now, that's a substantial leave behind!

2.2 Don't forget cause and effect

It pays over the long term to stay friendly because the economy is a big wheel — whoever is on the bottom today may just be on top tomorrow. When the economy stalled with the savings and loan debacle, I called my printer, photographer, and writer and asked them to bear with me until I could turn things around. The printer and photographer were understanding and patient. The writer sued in small claims court for a couple hundred dollars. Within a year, I worked for a nationwide corporation and was responsible for all creative services. The printer and photographer got a steady flow of work for the next ten years, far more work than I could ever give them as a freelancer. The writer got a piece of paper from small claims court telling her she'd won her case; she collected only the same grief and embarrassment she caused me, but more importantly, she never got another paying job from me.

Think about the long-term consequences before you act. It's much smarter to work with debtors and be patient. Don't threaten lawsuits and credit tampering; that only increases hostility and decreases the chances you will be paid. There will be times when you're trying to collect and times when you owe money, so be considerate and try to work it out. But be forewarned — there is no risk-free method of doing business as an individual, short of working on retainer. Of course, if you see the person who owes you money driving a new Ferrari or shopping at Neiman Marcus, that's an entirely different situation and should be dealt with as you see fit.

When a lawsuit is filed, the only people who always make money are your lawyer and the other party's lawyer.

2.3 Avoid the final solution: The lawyer

Rarely is it in your best interest to sue. When a lawsuit is filed, the only people who always make money are your lawyer and the other party's lawyer. Win or lose, your lawyer always get paid (just like your stockbroker), and always out of your pocket. Whether you lose money or make money, the lawyer gets his fee.

Here are a few of my experiences that might help you decide what course of action to pursue for your particular circumstance. First, decide whether it's worth the emotional stress, dedicated time (sometimes years are involved), and money to pursue the wayward client. Is it going to take $3,000 in lawyers' fees and court costs to collect $5,000? If so, you may conclude it's not worth the trouble and chalk the whole thing up to a learning experience. Note that the statute of limitations on debt is three years from the date of the last payment or the date the debt was created, whatever the latter. After that time, the debt is uncollectible by legal means. This is not intended as legal advice, but a reminder that the United States of America was founded by debtors fleeing from English debtors' prison, and certain leeway exists in the collection of money owed. In other words, nobody goes to jail for debt unless it's for evasion of taxes or intentional fraud.

In Canada, debt collection falls under the *Limitations Act* of each province or territory. Depending on the province or territory you live in, collection of a debt can range between two and ten years. It can also depend on any court judgments you may have against the person owing. For more information, you should check the *Limitations Act* in your province or territory.

2.3a Example 1: The enemy ups the ante

One of the printers I worked with regularly referred clients to me, which proves the source can't always be blamed for a problem client. This client lived in a high-rent district and drove a new Mercedes. Rumor had it that her much older, rich husband suggested she find a project to get her out of the house and, at the same time, keep her from spending her days shopping. She brought me her massive assignment and I quoted an hourly rate. I kept a time sheet with detailed notes of my work, which I reviewed with her periodically.

If you choose to use a collection agency, plan on leaving at least 50 percent of the money owed in the pockets of the agency.

Frequently, she stood next to me at the drawing table, making her fourth and fifth round of revisions. I pointed out we were making arbitrary changes that made little or no difference to the quality, a responsibility all freelancers have when they see a client spending unnecessarily. I made a point of reviewing my time sheet with her at week's end as the project progressed, warning her of her accumulating cost. She was very pleased, told me not to worry about it as money was no object, and the job went to press. I billed her at the end of the month, halfway through the job, not imagining any problem with payment. The 300-plus-page book was printed and went into promotion. It sold, but slowly, and she started dragging her feet about paying. I called her as the invoice reached 60 days. Remember that delay coupled with the phrase "Money is no object" are two of the sure signs you won't be paid (see Chapter 9).

Clearly the work had been done, the client was pleased, and she could afford to pay her bill. Yet sales slowed to a trickle, and she was scolded by her successful husband for her failure; he told her to use her considerable monthly allowance to pay her art charges. (He was trying to teach her how to run a business — at my expense.) For three months, she delayed payment by reassuring me I would be paid with the incoming profits from the sale of the book. I hired a lawyer, who also kept detailed time sheets. My client called my lawyer incessantly, chatting about her bill and how the book wasn't selling. Oh, if only she could return the endless hours I had worked on her project, much the same as she returned a dress at Saks Fifth Avenue.

Sometimes after you've poured your heart and soul into a project and you don't get paid, taking the client to court is the only way you can live with yourself. When someone can clearly pay and chooses not to due to a preference for shopping at Neiman's, legal remedies may be necessary. If business is good and your client still won't do the right thing after sincere efforts to work things out, then court is a viable remedy if you are unwilling to walk away. Only you can decide if it's worth your time and trouble.

A word of warning: judges in real life are not like judges on television. In case you haven't noticed, US judges are also called justices of the peace. Sometimes they reach a decision that makes everybody happy and keeps the peace instead of doing what you think is strictly the right thing. They are, after all, voted into office. In court, I presented time sheets, the printed piece, and the signed proofs, and the judge told my client to pay the bill. Unfortunately, the judge felt my lawyer's fees were too high (increased by my client's lengthy chats). He ordered the client to pay only half the lawyer's fees. Guess who got to pay the other half?

Was suing this client the right thing to do? She wrote out a check in court to pay the bill, but after the judgment, had she not paid, I would have carried the expense of collecting the money owed, either by filing more motions in court to seize property, hiring investigators to locate nonexempt assets, or hiring a lawyer to do the same. If you choose to use a collection agency, plan on leaving at least 50 percent of the money owed in the pockets of the agency. Just a reminder of the way to avoid such a scenario: Work on retainer.

2.3b   Example 2: Appearances can be deceiving

My second wayward client was an engineer who started his own placement agency. If I had been smarter, I would have realized that when the price of oil plummeted, engineers were a dime a dozen. This might sound like a great opportunity to go into the placement business, but it's also an indication that employers will be laying off more than hiring. This man was referred by a printer and drove up in a brand-new red Italian sports car. He wanted a corporate identity developed and printed on the best of everything. It looked safe to produce this under the circumstances; I certainly assumed a man who could pay for a new car could pay for a stationery order.

He ordered logo design, blind embossing, and two-color printing, all on a number one text sheet, and he ordered in large quantities. Since it takes longer to order a die for embossing, I gave him a detailed production schedule. He said it would be no problem because he was going on an extended vacation to the Grand Canyon for six weeks and would be ready to start his new business in earnest on his return. Remember, people will decide the car payment is more important than paying your bill for creative services; and I imagine a Ferrari has a substantial payment.

Six weeks went by. The printing order was delivered and sat in my studio for two weeks before he finally returned my call and asked if he could pick up his business cards. I was suspicious. I told him everything was ready, not just his business cards, and he needed to bring a check with him. He asked if he could just pick up his business cards and would pick up the balance the following week when a big check came in.

Perk up here, because we're talking about a man who drove a car that cost more than I made in a year. "Sure," I said, "but you'll have to pay for the cost of the dye, since it was used to emboss the cards." He picked up his business cards, paid by check, and I never saw him again. Finally, he called me and admitted that he just couldn't afford to pick up the balance of his order. He confided in me that he had wasted six weeks on a vacation when he should have been developing his business. Though I sympathized, I sympathized more with the printer who had done all the work and owed his embosser and his paper supplier.

I felt obligated to pursue this client. I called my lawyer, provided him with the signed quote and the invoice, and filled him in on the details of the wayward engineer with the empty wallet, luxury car, and limited prospects. The client was served with papers to notify him that he was being sued. He didn't show up and I won the case by default. Does that sound easy? It's not. Even if you win by default, it's up to you to find the defendant's assets and go back to court to collect the money owed. Also, the court deplores a default judgment and will usually set it aside. After you win, you get to spend time and money to locate his possessions — such as luxury yachts, big savings accounts, vehicle identification numbers, or money market account numbers — and hire someone to retrieve them for you. This client petitioned the court to have the judgment set aside. His excuse? "I didn't realize I was being served. These papers were handed to me by some man while I was having a big dinner party. I just set them to one side and forgot about them. I had no idea I was being sued." Don't laugh too hard, but the delivery man was dressed in a sheriffs's uniform, carried a big gun, and wore a shiny badge. We went back to court a month later and the client wrote a check to cover his balance and my lawyer's fees. Would *you* have sued?

2.3c Example 3: Pursuing a debtor to court

My neighbor across the street and I were about the same age. She drove a Mercedes and came from a family who owned one of the oldest established restaurants in a major metropolitan area. (Recognize sure sign number two that you won't be paid?) She dropped by one day and asked me to design a menu for the family business. I was introduced to her brother, who described the half-sheet carry-out menu he wanted me to design. I quoted him a price and he agreed.

Though I make it clear that the client is always responsible for proofing the final draft, sometimes my desire to do a good job overrides the rule. In this instance, we flubbed the spelling on the famous American ice cream with the single umlaut "a" in the name and discovered it as the client accepted delivery of 5,000 copies. I apologized, told him I would correct it, and asked him to please accept the invoice I delivered with his order. He took the invoice and smiled as I promised to redo the menus and have them delivered by the following Friday.

Restaurant menus are low-dollar items, because most restaurants run on slim margins of profit. But in this case, it was the first job I had done for this client and I wanted to do it right. The menus were reprinted at my own expense and delivered as promised. After a long wait, the invoice was still unpaid and my calls were not returned. Though he ran the restaurant, he wouldn't come to the phone. Finally, I took a friend to lunch there. After lunch, when business had subsided, I approached him and asked about the unpaid bill. He told me he had no intention of paying for the menu, since the invoice was $30 more than he had agreed to on the original quote. Not only had I informed him of the extra charge for typesetting, but I had also paid out of my own pocket the cost of reprinting his menu to build goodwill. It amazed me that he did not hesitate to use the menu he hadn't paid for and saw nothing wrong with not paying his now past due bill.

When it's clear you're being taken advantage of, you either have to walk away and live with your decision or take some action toward righting the wrong. If I had been more experienced, I would have turned the other cheek and walked away with the menus in my hand. At the time, I sued this client in small claims court. His explanation for not paying the invoice was that he had no idea it would cost that much. The judge turned to me and said, "Did you apprise your client of the cost of doing business?" I smiled and reassured the judge I had indeed. "In fact, he received both a written quote and his invoice prior to delivery of the corrected menu, and if he had been proceeding in good faith, there never would have been a second printing to correct a typo, had I known he would not pay his bill." The judge turned to the restaurant owner and his lawyer, "Your client has behaved in bad faith, counselor. Pay the bill." I won the case, but put in the same situation today I would have handled things differently. This wealthy restaurant owner is a good example of a person who has no intention of paying no matter what kind of

Keep careful records and stop working when the retainer is used.

service he receives. There is no way to predict an outcome like this short of avoiding people who use and abuse others.

3. Tried-and-True Tips to Protect Yourself

Once again, the only sure way to avoid nonpayment for services rendered is to do what lawyers do — work on retainer. After you estimate the total cost of a job, ask for 50 percent up front. Keep careful records and stop working when the retainer is used. Wait for the next check before you recommence work. This may go against your grain; I know it goes against mine. Waiting for payment may delay deadlines, and it may make jobs hang on for what seems like forever. But it's the only sure way to overcome unpredictable human behavior.

You won't have to worry about collecting if you only work for people you trust or limit your creative services to major corporations. Remember that as a freelancer you are responsible for your income, and that responsibility doesn't end with finding the work. As one salesman was fond of saying, "It isn't a sale until the money is in your hand." You can be creative until you turn silly, but if you don't get paid, you're still just an amateur with a hobby. Spend time perfecting your people skills, and learn the nine sure signs that you're dealing with a situation that won't put money in your pocket (see Chapter 9). Believe your gut instinct, and don't give people the benefit of the doubt when one of the sure signs shows its ugly head. When you get that antsy feeling that says something's up, act on it. As a general rule, both parties should know a project is pro bono before you commit. The success or failure of a freelancer comes down to being able to advocate for your own well-being and trust your instincts while producing a spiffy creative product.

Chapter **11**

SCOUNDRELS AND SCALAWAGS, PIRANHAS AND BARRACUDAS

Are you keeping an eye on the ten other designers out there waiting to step into your place? Well, change your focus and concentrate on providing top service to your customers. There will always be people waiting in the wings to steal your clients by default or design. It isn't that we have an abundance of talented people jockeying for a few choice assignments. It has more to do with a lack of certification and expertise, so everybody who can calls themselves creative.

This is a well-debated topic, but like most other things to do with creatives, we reject organizations of all kinds. How does a client tell if the creative person he just hired has the qualifications to finish the job? A portfolio should be a good gauge of skills for clients, but frequently the work shown was a team effort and the person the client hired had only a small part in each project. If this *isn't* the case with you, speak loudly of your experience, but expect to run into more than a few scoundrels and scalawags who won't hesitate to adopt *your* work for *their* portfolios.

We've all met disillusioned clients who hired their last creative "professional" based on wonderful samples only to have the project turn out badly. Clients who have been burned in the past will call all your references, watch you like a hawk, and micromanage minute details. They won't really trust your abilities until the project is complete. Don't blame them — they don't trust their own instincts anymore, and it may take a little hand-holding on your part until they get over it.

Once you've gained a client's trust and proven your ability (the two main obstacles to doing business as a free agent), your relationship is usually clear sailing. You can concentrate on delivering top-notch creative service as opposed to worrying about politics, securing the account with niceties, or spending time developing a clear understanding of the client's goals and objectives. Your only worries should be the work at hand. Alas, in the real world, there are villains on both sides of the fence, and you'll find more than a few rich experiences in this chapter that you can learn from and, I hope, avoid.

1. No One Escapes Unscathed

There is no greater nightmare than being hired in the middle of a project because your predecessor mismanaged the job. You have to clean up, make up, and shape up the work enough to produce something the client will approve without tossing everything to the wind and starting back at square one. When you've cleaned up a few production messes left behind by well-meaning desktop publishers who got in over their heads, you'll know what I mean.

Powerful computers have created a new phenomenon: people who have little or no training decide they want to be creative for a living. It will take only a few botched jobs to help them realize maybe it takes more than a great computer, but the clients they mislead either knowingly or naively will still have the sting of a bad experience. You may have to start at square one if the job is really bad, but more likely than not, you'll be called in to rescue the client just before deadline. "Yes, well, we have this beautifully designed piece but it seems that it can't be produced. Can you help us?"

Be ready to accept partial responsibility for a poorly executed project even after you've done your best to clean up the mess. When the proverbial shit hits the fan, history has shown that everyone in proximity gets a little soiled. Clients who hire creatives because they dress right or have the latest equipment or come highly recommended by a nephew will ultimately pay for all those extra hours of hit-and-miss work. They'll pay by the hour for font substitutions while their pseudo designer plays with caps and lower case until he hits upon something that "feels right." Experienced designers study the delicate nuances of fonts and understand the systems behind building a good design. Though his hourly rate may be more, a bona fide designer will cost the client less in the end. And that person will design work that can be produced.

As you build your client roster and your success becomes evident, scoundrels and scalawags will be drawn to you like nails to a magnet. One print salesman was always very aloof and when business was booming, made a big deal about his expensive sports car. He invested in personal stationery with an eight-inch blind emboss covering the top half of his letter sheet. His name was all *C*s and *O*s, and even though he was an industry insider, he had raised enough ire within the ranks to motivate an unsporting tradesman to do the emboss upside down. He never noticed the negative space of the 300-point *C* cut inward where the *O* should have been on his fancy Crane's paper, but nobody liked him enough to clue him in. This same salesman supplied business cards to a major corporation when I took over their printing, and he charged the company three times the going rate for one-color business cards. As I shopped for vendors, I realized the company could get four-color business cards for his price. When I asked him to ship all the artwork to the new printer (who contracted to do the same cards for one-third the price), he volunteered his services at the reduced rate.

This is a variation on being caught taking advantage of a situation, apologizing, and hoping nobody notices. Unfortunately for him, the opportunity was already lost. What's the big deal about business cards? Well, the company had more than 5,000 employees, and that's a lot of business cards. Like the ten other creatives waiting to take your place, there were ten other printers lined up. Once somebody abuses you in a business relationship, don't hang around for more. Move your work to a friendlier, more hospitable environment that's conducive to good business.

Once somebody abuses you in a business relationship, don't hang around for more.

2.   Politics Makes Things Sticky

As a freelancer, you not only have to find the client, make the sale, do the work, pay the bills, and keep track of all your jobs' progress, it's imperative to keep watch for the unscrupulous scalawag looking to cause trouble. In an agency, part of the creative director and production manager's job is to shield creative staff from distractions. You won't have this protection as a freelancer, and it is not always possible to avoid politics, as the following story illustrates.

I had pitched my book to one ad agency for years, just waiting for an opportunity to prove my skills and act as backup for overflow work. One day, the creative director called and asked me to do a small production job. What he didn't tell me was that his favorite studio down the hall that usually handled backup wanted to charge too much to do the same job. He wanted to communicate to them (in an indirect way) that their prices were getting too high. He quoted a very small budget for the job and I accepted. I would have done the job for free to work with him, but I ended up paying with grief for the chance.

He told me I would meet the design studio art director at his agency for any changes or adjustments to the artwork. I picked up the type galleys and did the most perfect keyline (pasteup, for you young people) possible. My overlays were perfectly registered; my type was perfectly square. Nothing could have prepared me for what happened next. The art director looked over the boards and I made notes so I didn't miss anything. There were four minor changes and a tiny adjustment in placement. I came back the next day, and she gave me four more minor adjustments. The next four on the succeeding day just reversed the previous day's changes. My notes showed me she was just moving the same things back and forth for sport. I was being used. I had to drive ten miles each time this woman found another four things she wanted to arbitrarily change.

I called the creative director, explained what was happening, and asked for guidance. He reminded me that I had accepted the flat fee arrangement and he expected me to stick with the job, no matter how many changes she made. He was right, but he was also completely disinterested in the abuse, and I realized he would peg me as a whiner if I didn't shut up and do whatever was necessary. The next time I met the art director, as she requested each change, I pointed out the date she reversed that change and said I would be charging her for any further reversals. She suspected I was catching on to her and didn't want to push it.

About a week later, I got a quote from a well-known illustrator for an upcoming annual report. The illustrator I wanted to use asked me what I had been up to recently. I told him about the job from hell, moving things back and forth in a senseless tug-of-war. He asked me who I was working with on that job and I gave him the name of the art director and design studio. He laughed out loud because the guy who owned that firm had been in his studio picking up an illustration at about the same time I called him for a quote. The illustrator said all that designer could talk about was how his firm had lost a little production job that under normal circumstances they should have gotten and he was really mad. He was bound and determined that whoever did the production on that job would be sorry for taking that job away from him. He was going to teach that person a lesson. He had given specific instructions to his art director to make that production artist miserable. All he ended up showing me was the depths to which he would sink to for a couple of hundred dollars.

The creative director relied on the design studio for their services, but it was bad form to allow an innocent bystander to suffer as a result of internal politics. It was much easier to cut the freelancer loose than sever a reliable, though expensive supplier located conveniently down the hall, so who is the real scoundrel? The design firm owner who sets about to unfairly punish a competitor or the creative director who sets up the freelancer to teach his complacent supplier a lesson? Both parties are guilty of using others for petty gains.

The following story shows the strength of family loyalties, which can also cause trouble if you're caught in the middle. One potential client worked in the food services industry, where he always took great care of his customers (in this case driven by profit, not ethics). He asked me to design a rubber stamp for him that bore his monogram so customers would remember his name. I took it one step further and created a caricature that was an excellent likeness. He immediately fell in love with it and stamped it on every customer's parcel. I explained that if he only used this artwork as a rubber stamp, it was on the house.

Some years later, he went into business for himself. I stopped in to see him and he asked me if he could use his stamp in his advertising, now highly recognized by his customers after all these years. I said, "Sure, just as long as you consider me your advertising agency and I get to design and place your ads." He agreed, we shook hands, and I became a regular customer at his establishment. About a month later, I saw an ad for his business in the local paper. I stopped by to inquire if this ad had been prepared prior to our arrangement. He said no, it was prepared much after our agreement, but it was beyond his control. "You see, my daughter is in public relations and I have to let her handle my advertising." I reminded him of our agreement. Pay attention, now, as the scoundrel is about to reveal himself. My friend of many years said, "Well, it doesn't matter. I didn't put anything in writing." What he

A client who does not honor a verbal agreement cannot be trusted.

meant was, "My word doesn't mean a thing." Had he told me in advance about his daughter handling his PR, I never would have formed unreasonable expectations about doing his ads based on his promise. It helps to get the truth at the outset, but no amount of familiarity with your client can prepare you for a double standard.

3. Bottom Dwellers of the Worst Kind

I wonder how investors would classify management at Enron, the big energy trader — piranha or barracuda? These two pet names are reserved for people who draw blood and try to put you out of business. Whether their reasons are revenge or just a serious case of competition gone awry, they are dangerous and need to be handled carefully. I should note that the ad agency that gave me that losing production job also handled all of Enron's business advertising when it was one-quarter its eventual size.

When Enron started growing and took over a floor of rented space (long before it occupied the Enron Building in downtown Houston), the creative director wailed when they moved their business to a competing agency. He was visibly shaken when the other agency designed the new four-color logo and had it plastered on all their new literature. My friend, mad with envy, dreamed of Enron dollars floating just beyond his reach. When the mammoth piranha collapsed and left design studios, printers, and ad agencies all over town holding unpaid debt in the millions, my friend was overjoyed at his good grace, being only one of a few left unscathed. It's true when they say "Be careful of what you wish for."

Two barracudas who pulled a fast one owned a small agency on the Gulf Coast. They specialized in seasonal catalogs for shopping malls. I answered an ad for freelance help, and as is frequently the case, I wasn't above considering full-time employment at the time. The owner asked me what my rates were. She said that was more than she was willing to pay and would I consider a full-time job? Absolutely, I said, and asked her to fill me in. She said she had a catalog for a big shopping mall and would never be able to complete it on deadline with her existing staff. I accepted the job at less than half my freelance fee and worked as a salaried employee for the next three months, including lots of overtime. Call me trusting; call me stupid. Pay close attention and never let this happen to you. After the catalog was finished, I was fired; well, okay, euphemistically, I was laid off. Same difference. I had worked exactly 88 days, sometimes as long as 12 hours a day.

This barracuda planned to terminate me prior to my working long enough to collect unemployment and just short of the probationary period, when I would become eligible for benefits. She had saved herself significant money by having convinced me to accept the work as an employee instead of a freelancer. For $18 an hour and no benefits (instead of the going rate of $50 for freelance), she had gotten a first-rate art director and gained access to skills that had taken me years to accumulate. These are all very unethical things; but the lowest blow came when she told her clients she had to let me go because all of the work I did was unusable. I had samples to prove her company had used my work, but she was afraid I might be as unethical as she was and go after her clients.

3.1 A few words about noncompete agreements

When I was first starting out, they asked everyone at one animation studio I worked for to sign a noncompete agreement that would prevent employees from competing in any way for a period of two years after they left the company. I refused to sign it; so did one other guy who had worked there for a very long time. What happened when the other 12 people in the department signed and we didn't? Nothing, except the other 12 people thought they were bound by the agreement. Don't want to go to court? Don't sign away your rights.

The law regarding noncompetes has changed recently; now it states in so many words that an employer must get your signature prior to hiring, or he must offer you some benefit in exchange for this agreement. In other words, if you've been working for someone and suddenly they want to change the rules, they must make it worth your while with what the court calls "adequate consideration."* This is because signing a noncompete takes away certain rights.

Noncompete agreements are extremely difficult to enforce; even when they go to court. The court tends to rule according to the intent of the free enterprise system — that everyone is entitled to make a living. You may encounter a noncompete agreement when you subcontract If you really want to do the work, either hire an attorney to read it first, or read it carefully yourself, then make the changes that will allow you to live with the terms of the contract. Remember that a contract is only valid if both parties "come to an understanding" according to contract law. If one party doesn't

*source: http://www.bizjournals.com/seattle/stories/2005/02/21/focus6.HTML

understand the terms of the deal, the court usually will rule that no valid understanding existed at the outset, so it was not a valid contract.

There was a court case that resulted from an animation studio's noncompete agreement with an account executive. The salesperson found another job with a competitor in the exact same field and was sued by the company. The company sued on the basis that the sales representative was competing directly with her previous employer. The court ruled against the employer on the basis that one entity may not prevent another entity from pursuing their liberty to earn a living.

Finally, there is a big difference between a noncompete agreement and a confidentiality agreement. You may be asked to sign the aforementioned prior to working on jobs that involve the government or trade secrets. These are common and though they prevent you from showing the work you did to prospective clients, they do not prevent you from doing other work. Confidentiality agreements are common and do no harm to your rights as an artist or author.

3.2 "Work for hire" is a creative rights waiver

I am constantly surprised by the depths some people will sink to for the sake of money. Actually, I'm not that surprised anymore. My first exposure to the term "work for hire" was as at age 15. I worked part-time at the public library for one dollar an hour. Even at such a paltry wage, the head librarian couldn't resist taking advantage of cheap talent. She was close to retirement and spent her remaining days at the library writing a book on supervising library help. Though it wouldn't be a best-seller, it would be a book purchased by every library in the country. She asked me to illustrate her book with the understanding it was "work for hire." This means my wage for shelving books was payment in total for any artwork. Though I was underage and not capable of signing a contract, her publisher made me sign a paper saying I understood it was "work for hire."

Some years later, as a college freshman, I received a residuals check from the publisher for seven dollars, again plainly marked "work for hire." One thing you'll learn is that no matter what the circumstances, always do your best work. However, "work for hire" is a term you should familiarize yourself with so you don't sign away your rights as creative talent. When this term is used in forming an agreement, whatever you produce under these terms is owned free and clear by the person who hired you. If you are a photographer, logo designer, writer, scriptwriter, painter, or illustrator; you sign away your rights to control your work.

This is perfectly legitimate in day-to-day business. For instance, hiring a photographer to photograph a manufacturer's widget is a fair work-for-hire assignment — the rights to the photography and its unlimited usage is a fair arrangement in this instance. But if you design logos and do so under the terms of "work for hire," I will assume you have been kidnapped by pirates and are working under duress. A logo gains value and builds equity over time, so it would be smarter to arrange a different type of payment. No point in giving away the fruits of your talent and experience.

3.3 Your client relationship: Sacrosanct under the law

One printer I worked with gets the piranha prize. When my favorite printer retired, I had to find another source to handle some of my clients' stationery. The new printer was very inexperienced, struggling to establish a regular client roster. He worked with his brother, who had learned to run a small press in trade school, and they appeared to have a volatile working relationship. One day, a client called to tell me she had just had a call from my printer. She wanted to let me know that in the normal course of business, it was her policy to record all incoming calls. She stopped by my studio and dropped off a microcassette recording. I sat speechless as this man identified himself and proceeded to tell my client she could get the same services from him without going through me. (There are laws to prevent outside interference in your business relationships. If this ever happens to you, call a lawyer.) He told my client it would be better if she didn't mention the call, as what he was doing was called "torturous interference" [sic] and was against the law. He also wanted my client to know that whatever services I was providing her, he could provide at 25 percent less. I called my lawyer.

My lawyer referred me to a business lawyer named Fritz. Fritz was known around the courthouse by the nickname "Mad Dog," and I made an appointment to see him the next day. He listened to the tape and found it very amusing, especially the part where the printer said his lawyer was sitting next to him while he made the call. He picked up the phone and called the printer. Fritz told him straight out to stop calling my clients and warned him what would happen if he continued breaking the law. "You must be the world's biggest moron to not only break the law but also explain the law

Of all the things I've learned about being in business for myself, the most important is to focus on the work.

you've just broken. It's called 'tortious' not 'torturous' interference, and it's what you'll be charged with if you don't stop immediately."

The printer said he didn't know what the lawyer was talking about. Fritz was positively beaming as he said, "Oh, you don't. Well, I just finished listening to a tape of you speaking to one of my client's clients, yes, a recording made of you actually committing tortious interference." There was silence on the line and the printer, quite in shock, said, "I don't believe you." Mad Dog was quick to retort, "Oh, you don't believe me? Well, I'm not in the habit of lying and if you want to hear the tape, call back and make an appointment with my secretary ... and bring $200, because that's what I charge for an hour of my time. Don't expect to receive any money from any outstanding invoices, and in fact, it might be her name over the door of your business by the time I get finished with you. Tell your lawyer friend who was sitting next to you while you made the calls that his behavior would be grounds for reprimand."

The printer never called to make that appointment. Fortunately, he only did a quarter of my work. I didn't know how much damage he had caused, but I knew most of the clients he had called were fast approaching the no-spend zone anyway. The economy had slowed and most people were struggling to stay in business. The lawyer explained that a court case would cost a lot of money and take years to collect, and I would have to prove damages.

A situation like this is a lost cause. It's hopeless unless you enjoy spending your time and money with a lawyer who may or may not win on your behalf. Clients run at the first sign of impropriety, whether it's reality or fantasy, and people are quick to believe the worst about you, conveniently forgetting there are two sides to every story. If you find yourself in this situation, don't waste any time worrying about damage control. Abide by the mantra "The world is my oyster" and step into the next opportunity that presents itself. For me, a cushy executive position opened at a major corporation, and I can name one small printer who missed out on hundreds of thousands of dollars' worth of work.

Of all the things I've learned about being in business for myself, the most important is to focus on the work. Whether it's writing, photography, art, or design, your work is key. When bad things happen, either due to outside interference, circumstances beyond your control, or sheer stupidity on your part or someone else's, you still have your work.

When clients leave for whatever reason, it may take some time for them to realize their mistake if your work was excellent and served them well. They will have to spend time and effort rebuilding the same level of communication they just discarded with you. I recommend that both parties reconsider the good each entity brought to the relationship before ending it. (A clear line of communication with a gifted creative is harder to find than one might think.) At the end of the story, the greater loss is the client's — access to proven creative skills.

Chapter 12

SAGE ADVICE FROM A VETERAN

Mistakes are a natural part of any learning curve and if you're smart, you've already learned that you are a work in progress personally and professionally. One of the keys to success is getting up quickly after you fall — it's just like getting back on a horse. No matter how hard it may be to move forward, don't waste time rethinking things, building resentment, or plotting revenge. Pick up the pieces and move on. You won't find another client by sitting around tending your wounds or worrying about who's not speaking to you. Immediately reapply your energies and work to change your situation. Follow up a new lead, meet some new people at the local art director's club, or strike up a conversation with a stranger at the local art supply store. Remember that no contact is wasted.

When changing and learning stops, that's a sure sign you're dead. Most creatives fluctuate between freelance work and full-time jobs, depending on current opportunities. But the beauty of creative work, aside from unlimited potential, is its freedom and flexibility. Whether you cartoon on the side for a couple of glossy publications or strike up a friendship with an editor at *New York Magazine*, you can make a good living without an employer. You can also avoid the big-business concerns of payroll, employment taxes, workers' compensation, or providing benefits attractive enough to pull in talent.

If you want to keep your business simple, stick to using contract workers and peers to pick up the slack when you get a big project.

1. Step into the Future

With all the home-based businesses, outsourcing, and new technology, being an entrepreneur is part of social change. You may think you're just doing your own thing, but you're really part of the latest trend. Here are some quick tips to ease your transition to self-employment.

1.1 Create your own network

Many creatives build their own team models to support each other. They share experiences and discuss strategies that have worked in the past. Remember who you've worked with on previous projects and what their particular gifts are; keep in touch and add them to your resource list. Sometimes the politics at an art directors' club meeting are thick enough to repel. I organized lunches at a popular local restaurant where the famous rubbed shoulders with rookies just to overcome the barriers politics can construct. Many well-known art directors had long ago abandoned ties to their professional peers; the community was missing out on their accumulated knowledge. Our impromptu dates attracted them to raucous conversation, creative expression, and frank, informative discourse.

1.2 Subcontract when necessary

If you want to keep your business simple, stick to using contract workers and peers to pick up the slack when you get a big project. This saves time and trouble overall; and when things quiet down, you won't have to worry about laying people off. You've achieved success as a self-employed creative when you get great satisfaction from your work, pay your suppliers on time, take care of your clients as best you can, and forget why you ever wanted a full-time job in the first place. It's time to get some help — perhaps even hired help — when you spend all your time as an account executive, billing clerk, or accounts payable manager.

1.3 Read some business classics

It also helps to read a few business books, such as *Looking Out for #1*, by Mark Monsky, or *How to Master the Art of Selling*, by Tom Hopkins, to supplement your creative education. They are classics that prepare you for some of the more serious aspects of sales, build cold-calling techniques, and give great advice about navigating bumps in the road such as tricky salesmen, suppliers, marketing people, and secretaries who want to toy with your emotions and trip up your business. Though they address business personalities and selling in contexts other than creative disciplines, the message is clear, classic, and easy to apply and remember.

2. Artistic Respect and Freedom

Here's something to consider that plays a vital part in the success or failure of your endeavor and how you perceive it. I'm talking about the prevailing attitude hidden deep in the recesses of the noncreative part of America regarding theft of ideas and rationalized nonpayment. "This is an art form. I shouldn't have to *pay* for it." The young man who said this was commenting on the act of downloading his favorite music online without reimbursing the artist. This rather shortsighted point of view neglects to consider the artist's need for compensation for his labor; he will die without food, water, and shelter, and there will be no more music to download.

If you agree with his point of view, then don't bat an eye the first time someone walks on one of your invoices or illegally misappropriates one of your tag lines for his current project. This is only the beginning of how inadequate art education affects our society as a whole and how that nasty little idea of "I'm only in trouble if I get caught" undermines free enterprise. Until we teach people a reverence for thinkers and creators, there will always be ethical voids cropping up to nip us in the butt.

If creatives were more valued, our society would take leaps and bounds into the future instead of snail walking. We would be better off incorporating creatives into every level of corporate America just to introduce new points of view on issues previously seen as unsolvable. It's a good thing creatives don't need money to get motivated. When a society changes its values and recognizes that everyone's quality of life improves exponentially when creative ideas are put into action, things will change. The person who thought up and designed your watch is compensated or you don't get to wear the watch — that's easy.

When we convey the same lesson of respect and value to the source of an idea, issues of just compensation will fade. People will appreciate the value of creativity and pay the fare just as they pay for their Rolex watches without quibbling. "Idea people" dedicate the single commodity that is spendable once — time — on a client's behalf. After your lifetime is spent, there is no refund. More often than not, it is the creative who courts the muses and spends his "life's time" dreaming of ways to bring humanity a step closer to the ideal. Whether this time is spent inventing a better fuel or creating an original painting, the true expenditure and single commodity is time.

It is the illustrator who is faulted for drawing the patron with fewer wrinkles, less bloat, and no liver spots. That little bit of artistic struggle to push the bar up a notch sometimes interferes with presenting an accurate picture of reality. Creatives should be allowed to create without outside influence or deference; the flow is polluted when compromise is demanded or imposed. Individual vision is diluted when allowed to divert according to the vision of others; it no longer reflects the vision of the creator, an idea aptly put forth in Ayn Rand's *The Fountainhead*. If you can read about Howard Roark and understand his point of view, you understand creativity.

Excellent design cannot survive the politics of consensus any more than a painting remains the work of an artist if interfered with. A work of art has never been the product of a team effort. As soon as the work is made to accept more than the hand of one creator, it reflects a skewed purpose. (This is not true in an academic setting, where some mixing of hands-on wisdom may be necessary to guide the student toward resolution of the work.) There is no art borne of more than one mind, because the very act of creativity is one human sharing with another his vision and experience. How can you get inside someone's head to help that person show the world what he sees? You can't without inflicting yourself on that person's vision.

3. Cherish Creative Integrity

The lesson here for the freelancer is don't let clients insert subordinates between you and the controlling principal. It's great to have a secretary who can proofread, but only the guy who makes the decisions can tell you when the copy changes being suggested by others divert his goal or purpose. People can't resist inflicting themselves on whatever they touch — that's human nature. I've never met an account executive who could return an art board with the clients' changes and not add a few of his own suggestions, which he just *knows* will improve things.

Through power, position, jealousy, or ego, the untrained person is driven to mutate and deform artistic judgments based on years of accumulated training and experience just because he can. There's something irritating about spending your life in a nine-to-five job, moving stacks of paper from here to there without ever really creating anything. It makes people hungry to effect change somewhere, and they usually end up inflicting their frustration on a company publication. After all, they just finished redecorating their bathroom and it turned out just fine.

Each creative project compounds inherent knowledge and provides a reference applicable to future work. The lessons are so intangible and ethereal, even the artist cannot comprehend the depth of the lesson until some future problem screams for resolution and a solution magically rises to the surface. Creative growth is a massive endeavor; you must nurture pure integrity in a corrupt world to stay in touch with the muse that makes your spirit soar and ideas work. To know genuine resolution in art, your soul must be unencumbered by prejudice, personal preference, emotional lethargy, or laziness.

Laugh if you will, monkey boy, but great works are the result of experience, unbridled thought, and problem-solving. The secretary who insists on cluttering statistics with rules and boxes fights her designer in a desperate attempt, she thinks, to present her information *her* way. Far be it from the creative to explain that what she seeks is the comfort, predictability, and familiarity of an Excel spreadsheet, not good design. In business, the creative who gives in becomes easy to work with — amenable to suggestions whether they work or not and more likely to receive the next assignment. But where is his integrity and drive to improve readability and functionality? It has been replaced by a distorted purpose — the very real need to earn a living.

Then what has become of a higher purpose? This may be the real basis for the rift between fine artists and commercial artists. Fine artists and creative writers produce for the sake of their individual unadulterated vision and irrespective of the demands of their public. A commercial creative bends and twists his artistic skill to serve his client, but the bending must be controlled to allow that creative to maintain dignity of purpose — that ever-pressing need to think beyond the envelope, be fresh, and create something that's never been done before. The client knows his business, but usually knows little about the delicate nuances of design and font selection. In bending to please, are you doing what you're told or are you striving to give your client something that works? Sometimes you have to avoid undue influence from amateur opinions even if it

Sometimes you have to avoid undue influence from amateur opinions even if it makes the amateurs unhappy.

makes the amateurs unhappy. What depth of service will you deliver? Do you serve to satisfy only your clients' wishes and skip over your professional responsibility of providing truly creative product? Will you leave pride in your work behind, neatly tucked in your desk drawer?

Great creatives have always been hard to work with. Their standards are what make them great and, at the same time, impossible to live with. They have the courage to dream, work toward the unknown, and through sheer determination, throw their hearts and souls into uncertainty. Of course, they make it difficult for the mediocre to settle for less than they imagine and inflict a degree of shame on them for settling. Who wants to be around someone who is always pushing to make things better? Albert Einstein summed it up nicely when he said, "Great spirits have always encountered violent opposition from mediocre minds." But keep in mind something Albert Schweitzer said: "The tragedy of life is what dies inside a man while he lives."

Freelancing is the closest a creative can come to artistic freedom while practicing art to generate income. It is within your power to dramatically improve your client's image provided you don't limit yourself by bending to your client's wishes. Every time a creative gives in to a client's aesthetic preference, it restricts the creative's quality of work to the client's creative limitations — thus defeating the reason the creative was hired. After all, the client wouldn't need to hire a designer if he had the creative skills himself. You can work your way around a client's objections by taking the time to explain the basis for your design decisions. Most smart managers will follow the advice of a professional, but there are some who cannot overcome their desire to wield power in all areas — even in areas where they are ignorant. Many times I have prefaced my advice to difficult, controlling clients with, "Whether you follow this advice or not, you still have to pay for it."

Take the time to educate your client, and if you're successful in building trust, both of you will shine in the warm afterglow. Ignore this part of your responsibility at your peril. If you do, your work and sense of purpose will recede into the shadows as you become just another paper pusher. Though client education is not key to having a profitable business, it is the key element in determining a more important finale — integrity of a life's work and whether or not your creative potential is achieved.